FENCING
IS MY LIFE

Sergei Golubitsky

Fencing
Is My
Life

by
Sergei Golubitsky

Published by
SKA SwordPlay Books
Phone: 1.718.761.3305
Fax: 1.800.361.1379

Table of Contents

List of Illustrations

* Photo by G. Minozzi

"Float like a butterfly, sting like a bee."

—*Muhammad Ali*

I Dedicate This Book

To my mother, Galina, and to my father and coach, Vitali.

To my lovely, dearest daughter, Elena.

To Caro.

To my dear friend Daniel Boles, without whose support and help I would never have been able to write this book.

To Aurora and Maarten Jansen, whose family became my family in the Netherlands.

To Paula Papilaja and Chris Geurts for their help.

To Sebastiaan Borst.

To Sasha Tikhomirov and Snezha.

To Lena Sayenko and Anton.

To my teammates on the teams of the USSR and Ukraine.

To my refereeing "team."

To Mikhail Zolotariov and Aleksandr Perekalski.

To Vitali Ageyev.

To my former classmates.

To Vitaly Nazlymov.

To Steve Khinoy for editing this book.

To the Leon Paul team.

To Natasha Medvedeva and her son Sergei.

To the Reader

In the summer of 2000, I gave a training camp that was attended by members of Singapore's "Z" Fencing Club. Almost a year later, Henry Koh, a fencer from that club, e-mailed me. He told me that he went to a bookstore to buy a book on fencing—not a textbook, but a book with an interesting true story about fencing. He couldn't find anything. It turns out that there are a few such books, but I didn't know that then. That was when I got the idea of writing something down about my fencing career.

People have written about me as if I was bigger than life, as if I was an action figure. They've called me The Red Fury, The Terminator (sorry, Arnold), and Sergei the Terrible (like some monster). They've also called me Mr. Fencing, and they've compared me to the stars of the so-called "major" sports—Maradona in football (that's soccer, to my American readers), Michael Jordan in basketball, or my fellow Ukrainian Sergei Bubka in track and field.

And yes, I had results—more consecutive World Championships, more World Cup wins for the year's best record in top-level competitions, more wins in World Cup tournaments, than any other foil fencer in history. (That doesn't mean I was the best in history, by the way. You can't compare athletes from different times.) In my time, I was at the top—that's what you can say.

Writing this book, I can relive my fencing career from

moment to moment and share it with you. I want you to experience what I felt and lived during my training and during key tournaments so that you will be inspired to reach for the stars (as I was inspired by the fencers who came before me). I want you to learn from my mistakes and achievements so that they can find their own path to achieve the very best you have in you.

And by the way, I want you to have some fun, both while you read this book, and afterwards, when you fence.

Prologue: The Three Stages

Roughly speaking, there are three periods in most elite fencers' careers: when you want to, but you *can't*, when you want to, and you *can*, and finally, when you *can* but you're no longer sure you *want to*.

You can see these stages in me by reading this book.

At the beginning, you have a dream of fencing brilliantly, but you are missing a few things: the coordination, the strength, the technique, and the understanding.

At this point, the role of the coach or trainer is crucial. ("Coach" and "Trainer" are almost interchangeable terms, but not quite. A *coach* gives fencing lessons, while, in Eastern European parlance, a *trainer* is in charge of the whole of a fencer's preparation.)

> In Eastern Europe, a "trainer" is in charge of a fencer's whole preparation.

The coach (or trainer) has to make you believe that *your defeats and failures are temporary.* In fact, he has to make you accept that temporary failure is better than temporary success!

This first period in fencing lasts until you are ready to enter the senior ranks—normally, that is, between the ages of nineteen and twenty-two.

The second stage isn't defined by your age: it's the fruit of the years of dedication you've put in. If you start later than I did, this period comes along at a later age. Now you can control both your body and your mind. You know, very concretely, what you want and you know what you have to do to reach your goal. Your motivation is at its peak. You are living for fencing, ready to put parts of your life on hold for a chance to scale the peaks.

You just aren't quite there yet.

In the third stage, you have become an artist. Things seem easy to you. The impossible doesn't exist for you anymore; you solve all tactical and technical problems with ease, playing cat and mouse with your opponents. This moment comes to fencers at different times and in different degrees. For some, perhaps, it doesn't come at all. But if it comes...then almost always, at some point, your motivation drops off. You don't want to fight anymore, unless perhaps a tiger attacks you.

Folks, I've been there and done that.

And I'm here to tell you, *it's ninety percent mental.* You can only become your best if you find the motivation, and you can only stay at your best if you find some *extra* motivation, something that keeps you training and competing when others fall by the wayside.

Career Highlights

1985   Cup of the Ukraine (Senior): Gold Medal
1989   Team World Champion (Denver)
1990   Team World Championships: Bronze Medal (Lyon)
        European Team Cup: Gold Medal (Paris)
1991   Champion of the USSR and Spartakiad Champion
        Cup of the USSR: Gold Medal
        World University Games (Universiade) (Sheffield)
        Team Silver Medal
1992   Olympics: Silver Medal (Barcelona, Spain)
        World Cup Champion (end-of-season points
        leader in that year's World Cup events)
1993   Universiade: Gold Medal (Buffalo)
        World Championships: Silver Medal (Essen)
        World Cup Champion
1994   World Cup Champion
1995   World Cup Champion
        World Championships: Bronze Medal (The Hague)
        European Champion (Keszthely, Hungary)
        European Team Cup: Bronze Medal (Paris)
1996   Olympics: 6th Place (Atlanta)
1997   World Champion (Cape Town))
        Universiade: Silver Medal (Sicily)
                        Gold Medal by team
        European Championships: Silver Medal (Gdansk)
        Awarded Order of the President of the Ukraine
1998   World Champion (La Chaux-De-Fonds)
        European Team Cup: Bronze Medal (Paris, France)
1999   World Champion (Seou);
        World Cup Champion
        Super Masters: Gold Medal (Padova)
2000   Olympics: 6th Place; 5th by team (Sydney)

Reached the podium (first three places) at forty World
Cup tournaments and reached the final eight fifty-three
times.

At Home in Ukraine with Mom and Dad

Starting Out

It was March 31, 1980, in Kiev, in the Ukrainian Socialist Republic (part of the old USSR), on the last day of spring vacation. I was ten years old and a swimmer. I'd been in a swim program for four years, just beginning to train seriously, just beginning to be a finalist in my age group as a freestyle sprinter, dreaming of a first-place finish that still eluded me. (I remember, when I first started hard training, feeling that I was sweating in the water, that the water was burning me. It was all so long ago that it doesn't seem real.) That day, there was no practice. I was sitting home, bored. My father Vitali was a foil coach, so he decided to keep me out of trouble by taking me to the fencing hall at the Army Club.

Thanks, Dad!

I sat and watched while my father gave lessons. That wasn't much better than sitting home. So I took a foil and started to hit the wall target, just imitating what I saw the other kids doing. That felt pretty good, but somehow it wasn't enough. Then I asked permission to fence one of the kids there, another beginner—he'd been fencing for a few weeks. I won 5 – 3! I won! "A star was born!" … Later, when we came back home, I told my mom, Galina, that I'd like to fence. She was happy enough. I guess she figured I could keep an eye on my dad when she wasn't around.

Thanks, Mom!

But my father was listening. "No way!" he said.

15

I was stunned. I didn't understand for many years why he didn't want his son to be a fencer, but I finally got it.

For one thing, it's tough to be the coach's son. There's a lot of pressure, jealousy, and disappointment. I might think that if I failed, I would be disgracing the Golubitsky name.

Also, he knew—and I didn't—what a tough road it is to reach the top in fencing.

In our sport—in foil and sabre, anyway—you can only score a touch if the referee gives it to you. It's not like swimming, where the fastest time wins and that's it.

So for half of your career, you have to work to make your name, so that the ref will give you some of the close calls. After that, your name starts working for you—which is great, of course—but until then, it's seriously uphill. You'll think that you aren't getting calls you should be getting—and you'll be right—but you have to forget about it and move on.

But my mom and I ganged up on my dad, so that in the end, he had to give in. (Thanks again, Dad!) Then I ducked out of a tough one—I asked my mom to phone my swimming coach and tell her that I was quitting after four years. I couldn't bear to tell her myself.

That's how I went into fencing. As you'll see, it didn't get me out of hard training.

But let's go back in time a little bit to see the path that led me to this moment.

In the first place, I'm from Ukraine. Many people don't know much about Ukraine, because it was part of the USSR for so long and people think that it's part of Russia. Not exactly!

> In the first place, I'm from Ukraine.

It's true that Ukraine used to be called "Little Russia" and that it's where the Vikings settled and became the original Rus. But it has its own language and since the breakup of the USSR in 1991, it has been an independent nation of almost fifty million people.

When I was growing up, Ukraine was part of the USSR, the old Soviet Union. The top athletes in all the Republics got invited to the USSR team. .Ukraine was called a Republic. It was like a state in the US, except that many people wanted to be independent.

Ukraine had always been occupied by foreign countries: Poland, Lithuania, the Tartars and Mongols, then Russia.

The Ukrainian language was discouraged for centuries. For example, practically all education in Ukraine was in Russian, not Ukrainian—a sore point for Ukrainians. We studied all subjects in Russian from the first grade on. Only in the second grade did we begin to have a Ukrainian language class. In addition, all university subjects were taught in Russian. The result is that I speak and think in Russian.

(My daughter speaks Russian, too. But at least she studies all subjects in Ukrainian from first grade on. She even began to study English before she started Russian and French in the fourth grade.)

My father was born in Kharkov, Ukraine's second largest city with about a million and a half people. He was a pretty good fencer himself, but never got top results. The level of men's foil in Ukraine was always very high. The three or four best foil fencers were always on the national USSR squad, either on the first team or in reserve.

I've asked some "old" fencers about my dad. They all said that his strength was in tactics—he was a fox. But he had good technique too, being the "grandson" of the great Ukrainian fencing master Zakovorot. ("Grandson" refers to what we call our "coaching lineage." It means that he was trained by a master who was trained by Zakovorot himself.) So every time I fenced a tournament in Kharkov, people would call me Zakovorot's great-grandson. That made me proud.

Anyway, the time came when my dad was drafted into the army. He was called to the Army Sports Club (athletes got major breaks in the Soviet Armed Forces—more on that later!) and was stationed in Kiev. That was where he met and married my mother.

Mom had been born in Siberia, in a tiny village called Merkushovo, which is, in my opinion, in the middle of no-where. After the Second World War, her family moved to Kiev, because her father, my grandfather, had been born in a village near Kiev.

So Kiev is my city, where I was born on December 20, 1969. My city is very old—more than 1500 years old. It's called the "Mother of Russian Cities" because the first East Slavic state was established there—the Kievan Rus. Moscow was built much later, and St. Petersburg is like a "baby," being only a few hundred years old. Even though the Nazis bombed Kiev heavily during World War II, many beautiful historical buildings survive, like the thousand-year-old cathedral of St. Sophia and the great Baroque church of St. Andrew.

The churches were open but religion was discouraged in the USSR. My impression was that many priests were KGB informants. My grandmother and parents were bap-tized, but religion didn't exist for me, at home or outside it.

I was born in the Podol district, the old commercial cen-ter, just north of the oldest part of the city. My grandmother Tatiana, still alive at the age of 90, was lucky enough to be a janitor. This was a good thing, because it entitled her to get an apartment, and apartments were scarce in the USSR. How scarce? Well, in her tiny two-room apartment lived my grandma and grandpa, my parents and me (I'm an only child), my mother's sister and her husband, plus my little cousin Angela!

My father wanted to call me Spartak, the Russian form of the hero's name in the movie "Spartacus." This would have been a disastrously old-fashioned name. "Spartak" also happens to be the same as a famous sports club. It would have been like naming me "Yankees" or "United"—especially because I wound up playing for Spartak's big rival, Dinamo! Fortunately, a friend of my mother's talked him out of it, and I was called Sergei.

My mother is a beautiful woman (I think I have passed on her good looks to my daughter). When I was little, I remember waiting for the doorbell to ring, announcing that my mother had come home from work. I would run to the door, always expecting a kiss and a little present; and I was almost never disappointed. She always tried to get me the most popular toy or the clothing that was "hot" at that moment. I guess she spoiled me.

Now that I am grown up, my mother has become a good friend. We can talk about things. I find myself asking for her advice...much more often than I did when I was young and knew everything!

I was stubborn from the beginning. One of my earliest memories is playing outdoors with my father. I lost my balance and fell down. I wasn't hurt, I wasn't crying, but I said to him, "Pick me up—*now!*"

He said, "You fell down by yourself; you'll have to get up by yourself."

I threatened him: "If you don't pick me up, you'll get in trouble."

"We'll see," he said.

After a while, I gave up, got up, and went home. Mom was cooking lunch. I told her what happened—at least, my version. So when Dad came home, he got yelled at: "Why did you push little Sergei down?" I was four years old. I got my father in trouble, but at least I learned to pick myself up on my own.

As you can see, my dad was the disciplinarian in the family, as well as my coach. It hasn't been easy for me to separate dad from coach. His greatest contribution to my upbringing was his sense of justice and honor. I owe it to him that I have become a man of my word.

I started swimming in 1975. That was also when my father got an apartment and we were able to move out of my grandmother's place. We moved to an apartment

The habit of hard practice is an advantage that lasts! in a new nine-story building in a complex on the edge of the city. It seemed miles away from everything, although it was only thirty-five minutes from my old neighborhood by bus. In the end, I didn't become a swimmer, as you know, but swimming was good for me. It toughened me up physically and made me start to develop the character of a competitor. I think that this was my parents' intention —I wasn't a very strong kid when I was younger, though eventually I grew to the size at which I competed— just under six feet tall (1.82 meters) and about 180 pounds (82 kg.)

All the endurance practice—and the *habit of practicing*—served me well when, at ten years old, I began my fencing career.

Besides, I was left-handed. That's an advantage at first, because right-handers, who are in the majority, don't get used to fencing lefties as quickly as we lefties have to get used to fencing right-handers.

This is an advantage which, in time, diminishes to the vanishing point.

But the habit of hard practice is an advantage that lasts!

What I learned—and what I teach!

To beat really good fencers, you need technique. In my opinion, perfect technique is the most important thing for a beginner to master—or for a coach to teach.

That's the way I learned it—and that's why my butt was sore so often.

Here are some fundamentals that I learned early, and that I still teach all my fencers.

[All of these tips are for beginners (and their coaches). Advanced fencers need to concentrate on broadening their repertoire, perfecting their technique, and building up their physical conditioning, confidence, and mental strength.]

Learn to Touch Straight!

I had to learn to touch straight, with perfect accuracy. If we're standing at arm's length, it's hard to miss, but when you're delivering a full lunge or an advance – lunge, even a small error will ruin your attack.

I see some coaches who applaud if their student's attack simply arrives—anywhere, anyhow. This is just not good enough! In a lesson, the attack has to arrive at a precise spot, with the wrist in the correct position, and so on.

The En Garde

Of course, the very first thing I learned was the en garde and how to hold the weapon. This is basic, but very difficult for a kid to learn. The coach has to demonstrate and explain it over and over again—show what the position is and tell why it has to be that way.

I teach a deep en garde with the blade held relatively low.

In fact, I teach the classical en garde position—the feet at right angles, a foot and a half apart, the balance right in the middle.

Too much weight on the front leg, and it's too hard to lunge and recover. Too much weight on the rear leg, and there's too much of an "up" component in your lunge—you'd hang in the air instead of moving forward. Balance is very, very important. And you need to maintain this strong, balanced en garde not just standing still, but moving.

Touching

Touch with arm relaxed and wrist straight.

Footwork

Stay down, keeping your knees bent. Stay balanced in your en garde position throughout every move. This takes constant practice, but it's worth it. Off-balance footwork, no matter how fast, creates a weakness that a smart opponent can exploit.

The Lunge

I learned two different kinds of lunges: the "kick" lunge and the "push" lunge.

The "kick" lunge is used from short distance. You use it for one-tempo attacks—a straight lunge, or a lunge with a single disengage or coupé. The whole point is to be in the air for as short a time as possible. You don't use your rear leg because that keeps you in the air longer and slows you down. The kick lunge is made with an explosive kick with the front leg only.

The "push" lunge is more difficult to learn, and it creates more problems for the fencer—it requires more energy and is harder to recover from. Here you use the rear leg to propel you forward with maximum distance. Use it for compound attacks—usually two tempos. You can hang in the air a little longer, making an extra disengage or coupé (or even withdraw your arm at the start of the lunge).

No matter what kind of lunge you perform, you have to wind up with your feet exactly the same distance apart, and along the same line, and you have to finish with your back leg straight. This is all easier with the kick lunge, because your back leg stays in the same place.

Here are some ways to learn either kind of lunge:

Imagine that you are standing on a very thin bridge ... a narrow board ... a balance beam. Now lunge—and imagine that if your front foot misses the beam, you fall into a river where crocodiles are waiting to eat you! Or do your footwork along a line on the gym floor—with your eyes closed! Do your feet land on the line, or did you fall into the ravine?

You can also practice lunging *along a wall*— if your hand or arm goes out of line, it will hit the wall.

The Foil and How to Hold It

Holding the weapon sounds easy, but it isn't simple. My dad started me with a French grip, and I believe in that. In my opinion, you will learn all the fine points of handling the weapon with a French grip better than you will with a pistol. (Once you've learned the techniques, you can switch—but not before.) The French grip teaches you how to manipulate your weapon with your fingers, while the pistol grip encourages you to use your wrist or even your elbow.

The Disengage

You should perform the disengage with your fingers and wrist, not your whole arm. It's smaller and faster.

If you can disengage in half a second using your wrist, you can do it in a quarter of a second using your fingers. Any little bit that makes your technique faster and more accurate is worth it. It's like downhill skiing, where an aerodynamic position can shave seconds off your time and give you the victory!

If you don't learn correct technique from the beginning, you make your fencing future much more difficult.

A Finger Play Exercise

You can play "Catch the Blade" to improve your finger play:

The student and the "coach" (who can be the actual coach or just another student) stand on guard, facing each other.

The blades are engaged—let's say in four, but remember to practice this in every engagement. The student is pressing the coach's blade slightly.

The coach tries to take the student's blade from the other side (in this example, with a counter-four). The student tries to disengage and deceive the coach.

When I play this game, I can always catch my student's blade the first few times, and he tells me that there's no way he can disengage in time. I always smile, because after a few more tries, he'll get his fingers into the act, and my blade will bite on air.

The Parries

It's important to learn to parry with the guard or the "strong" part of the blade (the forte), and to make sure that the point is "looking at" the target—that is, not to let the point go too wide.

Don't parry too hard—instead, try to think about "building a wall"—that is, taking the correct parry position and not going beyond it. The wider the parry, the longer and slower the riposte! A wide parry means that you are still parrying when you ought to be riposting! Sometimes, when my student takes a really wide parry, I yell: "Trying to protect your girl-friend, too?"

I try to teach my students to pause slightly in the parry and only then make a lightning-fast riposte.

Finish Fast!

It's very important to remember this: the beginning of any action is slower than the finish, the final. Or put it the other way—the final has to be faster than the beginning. That means

- The riposte must be faster than the parry!

- The advance (step forward) has to be slower than the lunge or fleche!

- Sometimes you have to rein yourself in during the preparation so that you can explode into the final!

Don't Get Hung Up on the Flick!

I know that the flick is very popular. I like it and use it myself. But I don't think that coaches should teach the flick until their student has more or less complete technique. **Trying to flick too early can destroy your fencing** because you learn the wrong pattern of movement. Flicking is just one technique; it's not all of fencing.

I didn't learn to flick until I was nineteen. As I said, I like it—it's spectacular and effective. But by the end of my career I was flicking only about 10% of the time.

A complete fencer has to know every technique in fencing. If something isn't working for you, you have to have the knowledge and ability to pull something else out of your bag of tricks—the way a magician pulls the rabbit from his hat!

Five Years Old and Dreaming of Greatness

Self-Portrait as a Young Beginner

Fencing was part of my imagination before I thought of fencing as a sport. For some reason, swordsmanship was in fashion in the movies of the USSR when I was a young boy in the seventies, and my father—who knows with what dream in his head?—took me to every one of them. In my mind, the greatest of all the swordsman was Zorro, as played by the great French actor Alain Delon. I wanted to be Zorro the way another kid might have wanted to be Superman. So stage fencing, movie fencing, with its romanticism, its grandeur, its beauty of movement, was the source of my first inspiration to be a fencer.

In my dreams, I wanted to fence as brilliantly as my screen heroes. But the truth is that no young kid has that combination of coordination, flexibility, explosiveness, and strength...not to mention that in the movies, the hero

27

always wins. So it just wasn't possible at the outset, but the motivation, the inspiration, and the dream were there.

Much later, my imagination was caught by the movie "Highlander," about a Scottish swordsman who has to fight a series of immortal opponents, gaining each one's energy, force, and power. The trailer explains it all:

> *"From the Dawn of Time We came, moving silently down through the centuries…struggling to reach the time of the Gathering; when the few who remain will battle to the last."*

That seemed a lot like the world of fencing to me: there are a few immortals at the top of the fencing world, and you have to overcome them to become truly one of them. I wanted to be a "Highlander," like my hero, the great Vladimir Smirnov, who was a member of my club.

I fenced three times a week, and of course, I had to do my schoolwork as well. I would wake up at 7:15 every morning, do calisthenics for about fifteen minutes, eat the breakfast Mom had made me, and walk to school—an easy fifteen-minute walk, and I'd be there. Usually I came home for lunch about 3:00 in the afternoon, did some homework, then went to the Army Club fencing room. *That* was a tough

The days I didn't fence, I ran, building an essential base for physical and mental endurance.

trip—more than an hour each way, in a rush hour crowd so dense that sometimes I would find myself hanging in the air, my feet dangling helplessly above the floor of the bus.

I didn't get special treatment just because I was the coach's son. In fact, I had to address my dad very formally, as "Vitali Andreevich," using his name and his father's name—like addressing him as "Mr. Golubitsky" in English. And I got my butt smacked with the foil just like anyone else when I acted out of line or made mistakes. Sometimes, when I was back in school after one of these rough sessions, I would be squirming around in my seat trying to find a comfortable way to sit.

Lots of times I simply didn't understand what my coach was asking me to do, let alone why he wanted me to do it. It didn't matter how hard I tried or how mad he got at me or how much he hit me—I just couldn't get it. I'm sure that every beginner has had this problem. And it didn't go away in the first year or two.

Also, it was hard to get an individual lesson. My dad was in charge of several groups and I had to earn the right to get a lesson. But sometimes I was so sore already that I would do anything to make sure I *wouldn't* get one!

I can understand why a coach hits a student. Suppose you're giving a lesson, and the student doesn't get an action. You try, and you try, it doesn't work, you switch to another action. That doesn't go any better. You give a short break and go back to the lesson. It still doesn't work. At this point, you might think about hitting your student with the foil—just to get his attention!

I have to say that I've done this myself as a coach. (Hey, it works sometimes!) However, I no longer think that it is justified. The coach-student relationship has to be based on mutual respect and trust.

This respect was lacking in the system I was brought up in. Your coach screamed at you, and his boss screamed at him. You didn't dare say one word back to him, and he didn't dare to say one word back to his boss. The whole Soviet system was based on fear and control, not respect.

And Soviet sport was part of the Soviet system.

I wasn't good at first, but I was always competitive.

For example, almost every training session used to start with some kind of relay race. I used to love them. We would divide up into two or three teams, and Dad would try to make the teams equal in quality. I always wanted to win. I even felt that wasn't fair to everybody else because

I wanted to win so much. Every day, I would be on a different team, but every day, my new team would win the relay.

Many years later, I felt the same about my fencing opponents at international senior circuit—that I was beating them just because I wanted to win more than they did.

We used to practice for an hour and a half, three times a week. I have to say that it wasn't a whole lot of fun at first. We did endless footwork and target work. We worked ourselves into good physical shape. We did pair exercises. I have to admit it—it was hell. My legs were always sore.

We didn't do a lot of free fencing in that first year. I took that for granted, of course. It was the way things were. Now, as a coach, I let my students fence as early as possible: dueling, sword fighting—that's what draws them to fencing in the first place.

Worst of all, we weren't allowed to fence electric: we were too new and too young for that. Besides, electric fencing equipment was always in short supply, even in the great Soviet sports system! So we watched the senior fencers fencing electrically with the scoring lights, and we dreamed that we would fence electric like them some day.

After practice, I'd take a cold shower. That wasn't my choice; it was just that hot water was in short supply! Then, sore and tired, I'd take the bus home.

I'd get home around eight o'clock in the evening. If I had finished my homework, I had a few minutes of free time after dinner. If not, it was homework time. I was in bed by ten.

The days I didn't fence, I ran. This built an essential base for physical and mental endurance. I wasn't too enthusiastic about it at first, but soon I got used to it and it stopped bothering me. In fact, after a while, I felt worse if I had to skip running. I'd run about a half hour or forty-give minutes a day, rain or shine.

I used to run in the woods outside Kiev. I loved to run alone. I felt like Rocky in the movie, running alone to that great music, even though I hadn't seen the movie yet. I felt that I was paying for success by suffering while my rivals were taking it easy. But most of all, while I was running, I let my mind rest.

Sometimes I would run to a certain place in the forest, then turn around and run home. Other days, I stopped at that spot and did stretching and footwork before running back. Some days I ran fast, some slow, some mixed. In other words, I ran the way I felt that day.

Once, in the middle of winter, I took a wrong turn and got lost. The temperature was -25^0C. (that's thirteen below zero Fahrenheit). It took me more than an hour to find my way back home.

In retrospect, it's hard for me to explain why I put up with this endless training. Part of it is simply my character and the discipline that my father instilled in me.

Partly, I think it was the Soviet mentality at that time. If you go out for a sport, you have to become a World Champion for the sake of the USSR!

I believed in that. I was patriotic. And I think it's a good thing. It's important for any nation that its kids grow up wanting to do well for the sake of their country, and believing that they will do well because they are from their country.

I think that Americans are like that, too. That's why, when they are fencing, even when they don't have the same technical level, their character and national mentality gives them extra strength. (The Russians are still like that.)

There was another reason for all the hard work. I wasn't conscious of it as a ten year old, but it was there just the same. For a Soviet citizen (and still for the Cubans and Chinese), one of the only chances to have a better life was through sport. You could get better food, a better apartment, a car (almost impos-

> It's important that kids should want to excel for the sake of their country

31

sible then for an ordinary human being), or even travel abroad!

Don't forget that we had an Iron Curtain. To get through it was no easy thing.

It wasn't easy living in the same house as my coach. I couldn't just roll out of bed and go to school like everyone else. Dad made sure that every day, before breakfast, I got some exercise in—stretching and push-ups. Whoopee! Plus I had to watch my weight and not eat extras.

It was only when Dad slept late that I could sneak out of bed into the kitchen and enjoy my breakfast in peace and quiet.

If he was reading the paper in the living room, there I'd be, poor hungry me, tiptoeing to the refrigerator ... opening it very slowly ... taking two or three minutes to open the thing ... and the stupid door would give out a traitorous squeak of alarm, and I'd hear, "Sergei, close the fridge!"

The sacrifices we make for sport!

Or maybe it would be summertime: school's out, everyone is having fun. My classmates are sitting with their girlfriends, playing the guitar, and I'm out running ... and they're laughing at me, making stupid motions to imitate a fencer. Ha ha ha.

Personally, I didn't have a lot of time to socialize at this time. But I had buddies from my school classes, from my neighborhood, and from fencing. I never felt isolated. I had two worlds—regular life and sport, which were each very satisfying, but different.

Plus my dad kept an eye on me. He wanted to make sure that I never got bad grades in school. And I didn't. In fact, my grades were excellent. Sometimes I even went out for the math or chemistry Olympiads for my school, where we would compete with other teams in solving difficult problems.

It was tough then, but looking back at it, it was a time of investment. I was building my base. If I gave everything, maybe I could achieve something.

I must have been doing something right, because I survived my first year, along with a couple of other kids from my group, and was promoted from the beginners group. Now I got to train with some of my father's older fencers. Now the training was up to three hours a day, three times a week. I came home later and more tired. But somehow I liked it. The older fencers used to beat up on me at first, but I didn't mind (even though I wanted to win)—I took it for granted that these defeats were part of the dues I had to pay. And gradually, I started to be trouble for them. They had to suffer if they wanted to beat me!

It's very important to train alongside heroes and role models, people who can help and inspire you. Your special role model can be a magnet for you, pulling you along by sheer force to follow in his or her footsteps.

I was lucky to have a great fencer in my club—my hero, Vladimir Smirnov, who won the 1980 Olympics in Moscow, the year I started to fence, and the World Championship in 1981 in France. His career was cut tragically short during the men's foil team event at the 1982 World Championship in Rome. The USSR was fencing West Germany, Smirnov against Matthias Behr. As the two men came together, Behr's blade broke, and the sharp stump pierced Smirnov's mask, entered his left eye, and went straight into his brain. The doctors kept him alive for two days, but he was brain dead. The whole fencing world mourned.

Don't get the impression that fencing is a deadly sport! There were only seven recorded fatalities in the twentieth century, plus one in 2004—all but one among elite fencers. Safety equipment has been greatly improved since Smirnov's death.

Injuries like this don't happen among very young fencers because kids don't have the strength to generate the tremendous forces required for such a terrible event to happen.

After the accident, the fencing rules were changed to require stronger masks, and uniforms made of ballistic material, and blades made of Maraging steel, which lasts longer and doesn't break off sharp when it does break.

On the way to our fencing club, I always used to walk through the Alley of Glory. It was outdoors, lined with pictures of the greatest Ukrainian athletes, including Smirnov. One day, my dad and I stopped in front of Smirnov's picture. Dad said to me, "Sergei, let's swear in front of Vladimir that we will go all the way to the top, whatever it takes."

I had only seen Smirnov once in my life, but he was my club mate and my hero.

I swore.

I hope I didn't let you down, Dad, Vladimir.

Thanks, guys.

Let me show you how far my father was willing to go to get me to the top: he was willing to give me up instead of keeping me for himself and perhaps make me a victim of his own ambitions. One day he told me that he wasn't sure that he could teach me everything that an elite fencer needs. He asked me to talk to Smirnov's former coach, Victor Bykov. I was excited at the idea of being coached by the man who had trained my hero.

What I didn't know was that he had been twisted by the System. Like many athletes and coaches, he couldn't leave the USSR—some because people had informed against them, others because they were Jewish. Soviet sport was a world of dirty intrigues. Bykov was trying to compensate for his inability to travel abroad.

We entered Bykov's office. He looked at me from behind his desk with a satisfied look on his face, as if he had won a victory he had been waiting for: I was begging for something from him.

He asked me what my goal was.

I said, "An Olympic medal."

He asked, "What else?"

I said, "Another Olympic medal!"

He asked, "What's in it for me?"

I was stunned, speechless. Dad and I were certain that he was asking for a financial deal in advance—to bring back some gifts from abroad for him, or to take some goods from him, like blades or caviar, and bring him the money. Deals like this were common under the system, but we didn't want to play the game this way.

Without saying another word, we turned and left the room.

I'm grateful to my fate that I didn't change coaches and give myself to that man!

But, as you'll see after a few years, Bykov wasn't finished with me …

It used to be that lefties had a big advantage. True left-handers are only about 10% of the population, so they got used to fencing righties, while right-handers felt awkward against lefties. So there are a higher proportion of left-ies in fencing than in everyday life. I don't think that the advantage is as strong anymore. It's a kind of fairy tale or superstition. Coaches now give lessons both right-handed and left-handed (I do this myself), so that student fencers get used to both.

What remains true, however, is that lefties still have trouble with other lefties!

There was a kid named Aleksandr in from the Spartak club who had started about the same time that I did. He was a right-hander (I'm left-handed, remember!), taller and faster than I was, and for three whole years, he beat me every time we fenced.

Aleksandr was the top fencer in our age group. He had an incredibly fast advance–lunge, considering his age; it was simple but very effective. Meanwhile, I was always improvising—trying to win by better timing, not by planned action. He would always win, and I would place second or third.

I had just turned thirteen, in January 1983, when I had to fence in the Kiev Junior Championship. That was a big deal for me at that time, as you can imagine. My father woke me up very early on the day of the competition.

"How are you feeling?" he asked.

"Not bad, but I've got a stomach ache."

"That's just nerves," he told me. "You're a little scared. It's normal."

Much of the day is hazy in my mind, but one thing I know for sure. I beat Aleksandr for the first time. I was city champion!

The same night, they rushed me to the hospital and took out my appendix; I got complications from the anesthetic, and wound up with pneumonia.

But a few weeks later, I was taking lessons again—sitting on a chair. The doctors had said that I couldn't train, but by this time, I was hooked. I couldn't stand a day without fencing.

Cadet Years

The first hint that I had a real future in fencing came in 1984 (I'd now been fencing for nearly four years). I had done all right in the Cadet Championship of Ukraine — just well enough to qualify for the USSR Cadet Championship, hundreds of miles from home, in Kazan, on the Volga River east of Moscow. I had to go without my father. I was a complete unknown among many strong fencers, most of whom I was now seeing for the first time in my life. Let me tell you, it wasn't appendicitis this time — I was really scared. I have no idea how I did it, but I finished fourth. I lost 10 – 9 in the semis to the eventual winner, and also lost the third place bout by the same score. Not bad for the first time out! The coaches of the USSR team took notice of me and I was invited to some USSR national camps. It was the start of something big.

From My Journal

From here on, you will start seeing a lot of numbers, names, and scores. I want to show you how hard I had to work to get the results I got, and to give you some idea of the frequency of tournaments and travel, the intensity of camps.

It's not as if I have a photographic memory for all this information. It's from my training Journal. Every fencer needs to keep a record of every training session — how much you practiced, what you learned, how hard you

> **Every fencer should keep a journal. Record every training session, every bout, every opponent!**

trained, how you felt physically and mentally—and keep a record of every tournament bout against every opponent.

My first USSR camp was held in Odessa, a famous and beautiful city on the Black Sea, in the south of Ukraine, at the end of September 1984. I had been to training camps back home, but I was still nervous because of the honor and the responsibility of representing Ukraine at a national camp.

At the camp, I started to make the acquaintance of fencers from many different regions of the USSR. I was literally rubbing elbows with them, eight or ten in a room, sharing a toilet and a shower. That *one* toilet showed me the meaning of the Three Musketeers' motto, "All for *one* ... and one for all!"

Seriously, I learned a lot at that camp. I learned that people from different Soviet republics are different. We weren't all the same "Soviet men." Some of us could speak perfect Russian; others couldn't speak good Russian at all. Plus I learned that people from different countries have different mentalities.

Some of the people in that first camp have achieved important results. Valery Novikov beat me 10 – 9 in Kazan, in the semifinal, and won that USSR Cadet Championship, as you'll read later on. Andrei Pavlov and Pavel Soloviev made the top eight of the Junior World Championships in São Paolo. Elena Grishina was a major international competitor—she made the Olympics, the World Championships, and now works for the sports channel on Russian TV.

You never know what your camp-mates will become—or what *you* will become!

At that camp, for the first time, I was learning new techniques in individual lessons from someone besides my father—a Russian coach, not a Ukrainian.

My father had been training me in footwork, and to *feel* the blade, feel the timing of my actions—for example, that I had to finish *faster than I started*. The Russian system is more schematic and programmed (this is both good and bad!) I learned to do *pre-planned actions*.

Both aspects of fencing are necessary, and I was very lucky to be trained in two different visions of fencing—my father's and the Russians.

The basic principles of training were the same, but everything still seemed new and different—the footwork combinations, the details of the sessions. I was trying to outdo fencers a few years older than I was. I was younger than most of the other fencers and losing to them because they were stronger and faster. I was burning way too much energy, trying too hard. After five days, I sprained my ankle and had to stop training.

There is such a thing as trying too hard. This was a problem that haunted me throughout my career, as you will see.

Nevertheless, that camp was very important to me. It gave me a new sense of direction and new goals. Now I understood that I had to catch up with fencers from all over the Soviet Union. It wasn't going to be enough to compete only with my Ukrainian rivals.

I remember one other thing from that camp. I was with some of the older fencers, mostly girls, as it happened. We held a séance around a homemade Ouija board made of a plate set on a tabletop. You each put your fingers on the plate, then summon the spirit of a dead person. The idea is that if the spirit answers, the plate moves. It wasn't my idea, but they called the spirit of Smirnov.

And the plate moved!

Turning fourteen made me eligible for both junior and senior competitions. I got consistently good results as a cadet in Ukraine, practically always making the podium. But at Soviet Junior and Senior competitions, I was taking places anywhere from twentieth to one hundredth. Everything has its own time ...

In 1984, I went to quite a number of camps, growing more and more confident. The teachers at my school hardly remembered my face anymore, but they got to see my name in the newspapers.

I even started to make some money—like US $15.00 per month! I never paid for lessons, equipment, travel, and so on. And I was making real, Western money at the age of fourteen, which wasn't possible for non-athletes my age. I was living my sport.

So, with $15.00 a month, I was a "professional," a full-time member of the "Soviet sports machine!"

It felt good. You could travel within the Soviet Union and even hope to travel abroad someday, which no ordinary citizen could do. People respected you for being an athlete, more than for being a teacher or a worker.

At the same time, it was tough. To begin with, I was traveling from camp to camp, from city to city, mostly on long train rides. That was a strain in itself.

> **Camps would have three-a-day workouts one day and two-a-day workouts the next.**

At a camp, there would be three-a-day workouts one day and two-a-day workouts the next, with one day off each week. We would get up at 7:00 a.m. and go to the first session, usually fifteen or twenty minutes of running (just to warm up!) followed by stretching, fencing footwork, and then some strength exercises like push-ups and pull-ups.

(Notice that we warmed up before we stretched out. There's no point in stretching before the muscles are warm enough. Also, notice that in the "Soviet sports machine," our strength training used mostly body-weight resistance. We didn't have many weight machines.)

At 8:45 a.m., it was finally time for breakfast. This wasn't

40

just a "Continental breakfast" of a glass of juice and some bread and jam—we needed some serious energy! Then we could collapse back into our beds, savoring each moment before the next session. Our bodies still weren't awake, but they were already tired!

The second session would start at 10:30 a.m. We warmed up (again), stretched out (again), did footwork (again), took a half-hour lesson … fenced fifteen or twenty five-touch bouts, showered … and finally … went to lunch! This would be around 1:00 p.m.

Usually after lunch, we would sleep for an hour or so. They didn't make us—we needed to! We were trying to recover for the next session, the next day.

The third session, which was held only every other day, might be fencing or football (soccer). The session would run from 5:00 to 7:00 p.m.

I didn't think that there was anything unusual about this. It was just the way it was, from one camp to another … and another...and another.

But if Soviet fencing was strong during this period (and it was!), one reason was that the top fencers had to beat countless rivals who had been toughened in these training sessions.

I think that these camps were necessary, up to a point. You get tougher away from home, from your daily routine, from fencing the same people all the time. Besides, you can't train three times a day at home.

Of course, the other side of this is that in the Soviet system at that time, you were always on the edge of over-training.

A Landmark

On November 24, 1985, I fenced in the Senior Cup of Ukraine. It was held in Kharkov, my father's home town. After my year of intensive training at fencing camps, I was amazed—I could beat the best seniors in Ukraine, who were five or ten years older than I was! I won the tournament and was proud and happy for myself ... and happy for my dad.

Down to Earth

Then, the next month (December 1985), I fenced in a Senior USSR Cup. Whoops! I was a much more realistic forty-third. Boris Koretski won that event. He was twenty-five years old and a member of the senior Soviet team. There is no way to convey how far above me he seemed to be. He was unreachable—he used to fence with Vladimir Smirnov! He was totally unaware of my existence, like all the other "Highlanders" at that time! And he could *travel abroad!* If someone had told me that in four years, I would be with him on the USSR first team, I would have cracked up laughing!

But that's what happened...

My progress as a cadet continued—one step forward, one step back. I won a genuinely strong senior USSR tournament on April 11, 1986; and the very next week, I placed fourth at the senior championship of Ukraine. OK, I said to myself—I'm one of the top five in Ukraine, at least.

In June, though, at the USSR Championship in Leningrad (now St. Petersburg again) I placed a very disappointing *ninety*-fourth, and my Ukraine team placed eleventh among seventeen teams.

One reason I'm telling you this is to remind you that **the results of any given tournament don't mean much.** You need to think about your long-term goals and your total training plan.

Junior Years

Trying for the Spartakiad

In 1986, I graduated from the cadet ranks (sixteen and under) to the juniors. I was competitive against seniors too—but only in Ukraine. The truth is that after the tragic death of Smirnov, the level of foil in Ukraine had fallen. Smirnov was gone, and some of the other top fencers had retired. I didn't take this development as entirely bad news. It meant that maybe I could make the Ukrainian team for the Spartakiad of the USSR.

The Spartakiad—named after the heroic gladiator Spartacus, who revolted against the mighty Roman Empire—used to be the biggest event in the sports cycle of the Soviet Union. It was the Soviet Olympics: each of the fifteen republics sent its best in every sport.

I had good reason to expect to be named to the team. I was ranked second in points in Ukraine, and my level of fencing was high enough. But two months before the competition, there was a sudden change in the coaching staff.

Formerly, the coaches were Vasily Stankovich (a great foil fencer, a former World Champion, and a fine person) and Semyon Leshiov, my future coach at the University. Suddenly, they were replaced—by Bykov. Remember him? He was the guy who had asked me what was in it for him if I became a champion.

My father understood the politics better than I did.

He shook his head: "You can forget about the Spartakiad team! Bykov will never let you make the team, no matter how much you deserve it."

"I'll make him take me."

My father was worried about my state of mind. I had had a breakout season and taken my place among the senior fencers. He was sure that I was going to be robbed of my place on the team and worried that it would break my spirit and my self-confidence.

But I was stubborn. Anyway, what could I do but try?

Two training camps were needed to qualify for the Spartakiad. The first was in the foothills of the legendary Caucasus Mountains, at the resort town of Kislovodsk in southern Russia. It lies between the Black Sea and the Caspian Sea, near the current trouble spot of Chechnya. It's a beautiful place, with green, misty hills, but I wasn't enjoying the scenery.

From my Journal:

"We had sixteen days of training. I felt sick from the beginning of camp. Flu, nosebleeds, sore knees...."

And Bykov kept looking for a reason to leave me off the team.

We had a series of intra-squad competitions. The standings would determine the Spartakiad Team. My job was to make the podium every time—and not only that, but to place as high as possible. That way, Bykov wouldn't have a chance to throw me off the team. Only five fencers would make it.

From my Journal:

July 27: Three training sessions, sixteen 5-touch bouts. Fourth place.

44

August 3: Two training sessions, ten 5-touch bouts. First place (tie).

August 4: Three training sessions, 8 5-touch bouts, then five 10-touch bouts. First place.

Then we moved to the second camp, in my father's home town of Kharkov. It was going to be seventeen days of hell, with seven days of 3-a-day sessions. There was one day off. I didn't take it; I trained instead.

From my Journal:

August 22, afternoon session: thirteen 5-touch bouts. Third place.

August 22, evening session. Six 10-touch bouts. First place.

But then …

August 27th: six bouts of 10 touches. <u>Fifth place.</u>

This was my single worst result in a month of intensive training. It gave Bykov the pretext he needed. He picked five other fencers and sent me home.

I hadn't made the Spartakiad team.

I wasn't crushed. At least my father had warned me. But I was deeply disappointed just the same. I had wanted so much to represent Ukraine, to wear the beautiful blue and white warm-ups with the Ukrainian flag on the chest and "Ukraine" across the back. I would have been so proud to wear that flag … It was hard to let go of the dream.

But there wasn't much time to dwell on my disappointment, which was just as well. It was time to start another season.

1986—1987: Lessons from Losses

In September of 1986, within a few weeks of my Spartakiad disappointment, the training camps for the new season got underway. Looking ahead, I could see that I was still short of my goals. I was one of the best juniors in Ukraine—but as I mentioned, Ukraine was in a down cycle. I had a long way to go if I wanted to make the Soviet Junior team: I would have to win some national tournaments. That was way beyond my reach at this time.

However, I was allowed to train along with the Ukraine Senior team. I looked up to almost everybody on the squad, and the camp was brutal. They were trying to get us into physical shape for the coming season as well as giving us specific training. But I was in good shape from my summer, and I survived.

On October 3, back in Kiev, I fenced in an *international* junior event for the first time. There were foreign fencers—Poles and East Germans.

> The first time I saw foreign fencers, they seemed like space aliens. I was scared to fence them.

To me, they were like space aliens. They spoke different languages that I couldn't understand. For sure, they were stronger than I was.

And their fencing equipment was different ... and better. With us, only the members of the senior national team (and their close friends) had the expensive German foil points—the rest of us had to make do with the (at that time) heavier and less reliable Russian-made points. These foreign guys had German points on every weapon!

I thought I didn't do too badly, placing twelfth. But my father was furious with me.

"Every time you fenced a Polish guy, you lost!"

"That wasn't my fault—they were really tough!"

"No. It was because you were scared to fence them. You

walked onto the strip scared."

I realized that he was right. Looking ahead to fighting the foreigners, I had somehow given up the belief in victory. I told myself, never again.

The next day was the team event. I beat all four of the Polish fencers I had lost to the day before—plus an East German! I had learned that winning comes from a winning mentality—and that I could have the mentality of a winner.

It was a hectic season. Just two days after the Kiev tournament, I was more than 450 miles away in Moscow for a junior tournament—twelfth place. Then the team event on the following day. Then a thousand mile trip for a two week camp in the Georgian Republic, by the Black Sea. Then the train ride through the mountains to Yerevan, the capital of Armenia. (I beat two strong fencers, but went out in the third round.) Then it was back to Ukraine to train for the big one—the Soviet Junior Championship, which would give me a chance of making the junior team. This would be held on November 15, 1986 in the historic city of Gorky on the Volga east of Moscow. (This city was named after a famous Communist writer. After Communism fell in 1990, the name changed back to the original: Nizhniy Novgorod.) After another five hundred mile trek, I achieved …a disappointing tenth place finish, nowhere near good enough for the USSR Junior Team that would be heading for the World Championships in São Paulo, Brazil.

The rest of the year, I kept finishing in the top three of Ukraine Juniors, but I was getting nowhere in the USSR competitions. I resolved to train harder in the summer of 1987.

That whole summer I trained like crazy. I stopped thinking about goals. I stopped thinking about my standing, about my fencing future. Instead, I was making my future by training hard every day.

Toward the end of that summer, in mid-August, I became a student at the State University of Physical Culture in Kiev. It was a logical step to take for an athlete, except that if you weren't already famous—and of course, I wasn't—the first year could be tough. The professors wouldn't reschedule a test for you just because you had a training camp, or even an important competition. Many athletes from other sports had trouble with the first year, but I am proud to say that I stayed organized, studied hard, and budgeted my time well.

One course had an oral exam. I had prepared for it pretty well, but the instructor was making a joke out of the exam—she was really and truly *asking the students the color of the textbook cover!* And unfortunately, really and truly, many of the athletes couldn't answer. When she came to me, she was stunned when I responded that there were three important books on this subject, with three different colored covers ... and then I told her the names of the authors.

But many of the tests were more serious. I had to stay organized if I wanted to succeed.

On the second weekend of August 1987, I took part in Ukraine's Tournament of the Strongest, a senior tournament. It was a grueling two-day competition. Each day counted separately. I finished second both days and second overall. My hard work was beginning to pay off!

1987—1988

Then came another big breakthrough. Kiev was holding its international junior tournament again—the same tournament I'd lost to the foreign fencers and finished twelfth. This time, they had renamed it after Vladimir Smirnov. This year, I resolved to be tougher. I would have to be, because this year's tournament had a much stronger field.

I had a special objective. I wanted to show the coaches of the Soviet National Junior Team that I was ready to join the ranks of the top juniors.

And I wanted to show the home crowd that I was ready to continue the glorious tradition of Ukrainian fencing, and to do it in a tournament named for my hero.

> I stretched his legs, making him chase me the length of the strip until I found the space for a parry–riposte. A perfect touch!

It was a two-day event. The first day, I fenced fifteen bouts—three rounds of pools of six. I lost three bouts, but none to foreigners. Now I was in the round of sixteen, which would be held the next day. I wasn't only competing against by actual opponents on the strip, but also against the top Soviet juniors.

The second day format was direct elimination from sixteen, with repechage, i.e., a losers' bracket. That meant that you had to lose twice before you were eliminated. There were two opponents between me and the final eight. The first was one of the strongest juniors in the world—Ulbrich of East Germany. He got an early lead on me and I just couldn't close the gap—he stayed one touch ahead almost the whole bout until I finally evened the score at 9 – 9.

My last touch was perfect: he started an attack and I "stretched his legs," making him chase me the entire length of the strip until I found the space for a circle-six parry and riposte. My bout, 10 – 9!

Now I was looking around to see how I was doing compared to the other Soviet juniors. If I lost, they would gain ground on me. There had been eight of us in the round of sixteen and eight foreigners from the rest of the East Bloc.

My next bout was against a Russian left-hander, Dmitriev. I won 10 – 7. *I was in the final of eight!* I had never placed so high in such a strong tournament.

Another strong Russian junior, Ilmar Kuziaev, was the next to fall, also by 10 – 7. Now I was in the semifinal against Smirnov from Moscow. (I remember telling him, years later, that he would have to fence better or change his name—nobody with the name Smirnov was allowed to be a weak fencer. I'm not sure whether he appreciated the joke.) The score was 10 – 6, and I was in the final.

The only other Soviet left in the tournament was Gagik Oganesian from Armenia, at that time a student of Bykov's. I remember that as we watched Oganesian go onto the fencing strip against the East German Müller, my father leaned over toward me and said, "If you fence Oganesian in the final, you may have to die—but *beat him!*"

As you can see, my father, as coach, wanted to beat Bykov. So did I.

But Müller beat Oganesian, who wound up in third place.

I was the last Soviet left, representing my country, my home town of Kiev, against the foreigner!

I don't remember anything about the bout itself—I didn't write anything in my journal. But I do remember how I felt going in.

I knew that I *could* win. I felt that I *wanted* to win much more than Müller did. I felt that I had *no right to lose*. I just *couldn't* lose, so *I was going to win* ….

In the event, I won pretty easily, 10 – 6.

First place!

It was the best possible beginning of the new season. I realized that my dream of making the Soviet team for the Junior Worlds—in the USA—was not so distant after all.

Thinking back to the summer when I had worked so hard, I came to a very important conclusion: *the work you do is never wasted!*

I Switch Clubs

The USSR had three major sports organizations: the Army Central Sports Club, representing all the armed forces, Profsoyuz, representing the trade unions, and Dinamo, representing security organizations like the KGB and the police. Each of them runs thousands of sports clubs and holds its own championships. They are like three separate sports countries that compete with each other for supremacy and places on the Soviet teams in all sports. As you know, I started out in the Army Sports Club in Kiev, where my father taught. But our nemesis, Viktor Bykov, was making our lives miserable. He started sending my father to Kharkov for a few weeks out of each month, so that I couldn't train with him. There was no rational reason for this. I can only guess that he held a grudge from the day that my father and I had walked out of his office.

We had to change clubs if Dad was going to go on training me, and that meant that my father had to change jobs. Given the convoluted politics of sports, this wasn't easy, but finally we transferred from Army to Dinamo.

That is why, on November 2, 1987, I found myself in Baku, the capital of Azerbaijan, fencing in Dinamo's junior championship. I had just been notified that my transfer to Dinamo had gone through.

My father wasn't with me. I missed him, but the experience taught me that I could win on my own, using my own mind and abilities.

On that subject, let me tell you about my last bout before the round of eight. I was fencing against Mamontov from Moscow. I got far ahead, 9 – 5 in the ten-touch bout. But Mamontov didn't want to capitulate. Touch by touch, he came back to pull to within 9 – 8.

I backed up to my end of the strip, luring Mamontov into making his attack. I parried and riposted—but short! What could I do? I let out a huge yell of victory. Mamontov turned his head to look at the scoring machine, and I fleched to score the winning touch!

After that, I was walking on air. I cruised through the quarters, semis, and final, 10 – 3, 10 – 6, and 10 – 4.

After twenty bouts—three pools of five and five bouts

of direct elimination—I had won my second title of the season.

I was exhausted. Within the past month, I'd fenced three two-day individual tournaments and two team tournaments. Oh, yes—and throw in a hard training camp. But the USSR National Junior Championship was coming up, so I didn't take any time off. I went back to hard training.

Now I started to argue with my dad during lessons. The better my results got, the more I argued.

What he was telling me was the following good advice:

- Don't make the step before your lunge too fast
- Jump forward more softly
- Disengage with the point (blade) only, not with your whole arm.

And I was arguing with him!

I was beginning to think that because I had some success, I couldn't be wrong. Especially when I was tired or overtrained, I would take it personally when he would point out a mistake. Really, I wanted to improve, but somewhere in the back of my mind, I thought that my father just wanted to annoy me with pointless criticism.

Of course, I was completely wrong. In order to improve, or even stay at the same level, you have to be self-critical. Look for mistakes in yourself, and only then look somewhere else.

This was a lesson I learned the hard way. Other fencers shouldn't repeat my mistake.

It wasn't until I started my own coaching career that I realized how irrational I was then! My physical exhaustion was wearing me down mentally. I was keyed up about the championships, and it would once again be a long trip, this time to Yerevan, Armenia.

As a new member of Dinamo, I stayed with the team a decent hotel, in Yerevan. Imagine my shock when I went to look at the pool sheet and found out that I was still listed as an Army fencer! Somewhere back in the central sports bureaucracy, my transfer hadn't been recorded, so I wasn't officially a Dinamo fencer yet. I had to fence for Army. It was weird, but nice: weird because of the bureaucracy, but nice because I got to keep my hotel room, while the other Army fencers stayed in a cold barracks.

I did all right in the pools and made it to a DE (direct elimination) of thirty-two with repechage to the final of eight, which would be held the next day. I won an easy first bout against the giant Stepanov from Leningrad, but lost 10 – 8 to Oganesian from Armenia (the semifinalist from the Smirnov tournament). Fortunately, there was repechage, so I had another chance. Two wins later, I was fencing Pernikov from the Profsoyuz team for a chance for the final eight.

Being coached from the sidelines is not always an advantage. It is illegal, but many coaches (and referees) ignore the rule. Pernikov's coach was signaling to him exactly what actions to use. Since I could see the signals too, that only helped me, because I knew exactly what to do to stop him! So the coach shifted his position—he went behind me, where I couldn't see his signals. Fortunately for me, his fencer couldn't see them either, so he had to shout them—with exactly the same result. Final score, 10 – 3.

Next day was the round of eight. I won my first bout. Now I was one bout from the championship bout. I was up against Valery Novikov, whom I had beaten easily a few weeks earlier, in Baku. I jumped out to a 5 – 1 lead, then made it to 7 – 4. But Novikov was full of fight, while I still thought I was cruising to an easy victory. I wasn't ready to shift gears and paid the price of arrogance, losing 10 – 8. This wasn't the last time I would learn this unpleasant lesson.

I took the bronze, though—my first-ever medal in a USSR National Championship. And my Army team took silver. No gold …

In the following week, I took the train, first from Yerevan back to Kiev, (close to 1,000 miles), then from Kiev to Moscow (474 miles) and back, for my annual medical checkup, and finally from Kiev to Lvov in Western Ukraine (225 miles) for yet another training camp. Hours and hours of time gazing out the window of a railroad car, hours of time wasted. But that was the life of a Soviet athlete.

The next training camp, mercifully, was in Kiev. On December 19, the day before my eighteenth birthday, I left, with the Ukrainian team, to fence in the USSR Team Championship. I celebrated my birthday on another long train ride—this time to Riga, Latvia, where we would connect with a train to our final destination, Tallinn, Estonia. .

In Riga, a teammate named Bugaenko developed a terrible toothache. We rushed him to a hospital—where the dentist removed the wrong tooth! (Then he got the right one.) It seemed incredibly funny at the time to everyone except Bugaenko, and even he laughed about it later.

The team tournament took place the next day. At that time, the strongest teams were from Azerbaijan, Uzbekistan, and the separate teams from Leningrad and Moscow. We beat out Russia for fifth place, a big improvement over our eleventh place finish of the previous year.

The day after was the Soviet Union Cup, an important senior tournament and another chance for me to make my mark. I did well enough in the pools and won my first two bouts in DE. One of them was a good win over a member of the senior national team, Gegam Oganesian (not Gagik, my junior rival), before losing badly to Shvetsov, 10 – 3. One more chance to make the final!

The same thing happened to me that had happened at the Junior Championship in Yerevan a month before. I led against Fedin from Byelorussia and cruised to a 9 – 6 lead. 9 – 6! One touch away from the final of a Senior Cup! The thought filled my mind. It was all I could think about. I couldn't think clearly; I couldn't stay cool; my will was paralyzed; I couldn't move my legs… Needless to say, I couldn't score the last touch. I fenced like a novice and lost 10 – 9.

> The thought of making the final filled my mind. I couldn't think clearly. I fenced like a novice and lost.

It was an important lesson: *victory never comes by itself.* Sometimes you have to give more than 100% to score the final touch. Looking back, it was a valuable defeat. I finished in twelfth place and came home in a good mood.

After the New Year's Eve celebration at the end of 1987, I went running on New Year's Day, 1988. I couldn't give up a day of training! I would have worked out on the train back from Tallinn if I'd had the chance.

I had been named to the *Soviet* Junior Team for a World Cup competition in Hungary.

Even When You're Not Fencing,
You Can Analyze Your Opponents

As a Cadet at the Cup of the USSR, 1986.
I'm fencing with a French foil —
and I'm wearing the shoes of my hero, Vladimir Smirnov!

A Fencer in the System

The trip to the World Cup would be my first trip abroad. It's hard to explain what that meant—or how complicated it might be.

If you didn't live in the Soviet Union, under its version of Communism, you will never understand it. But I'll try to explain anyway.

Not just anyone had the right to travel outside the USSR. You had to be 100% "clean." And it wasn't simply that *you* had to have a clean record: nobody in your extended family could be a criminal ... or a dissident ... or a religious person who believed in God. People like that were untrustworthy; they were dangerous to the System.

And I have to admit it: I was a product of the System. More than that, I was a beneficiary. My grandmother was a Communist. So was my mother. And up to now, I had been taking advantage of all this.

Still, it was not easy to obtain a passport to *go abroad*. I had to go through many organizations, departments, channels; I had to talk with many big and little bosses; I had to undergo detailed cross-examinations. In the end, I was sitting before the last petty chief, the one who could finally sign off on my application.

He asked me, "What do you think of athletes who cross themselves before they compete?"

Understand: atheism was the official religion of the System. Churches had been turned into Museums of

58

Atheism. If you were religious, you were suspect. People were not conditioned to think for themselves.

I don't feel guilty about what I said, even fifteen years later. I was a product of the System. I didn't believe in God then, though I do now.

I said, without hesitating, "Crossing yourself is stupid!"

He signed my papers, giving me the green light to go abroad.

We flew to Budapest. Getting out of the plane, I felt as if I was going to see space aliens.

And that was also the beginning of a life of privilege!

After all, we must be special people, to be allowed out of the USSR. Many of my old friends had started to look at me with new eyes: I must be a very special, different person—a man who could *travel abroad!*

And I had *money* in my pocket! I was allowed to change 530 rubles into Hungarian forints.

At that time, within the Soviet Bloc, you could get US $1.60 for every ruble at the official exchange rate—and *only* at the official exchange rate. (Outside the Soviet Bloc, or on the black market inside the USSR, the ruble wasn't worth much, about twenty US cents.)

My family had never had real money—no more than anyone else. They saved up for me for ten years, and when I was sixteen, they gave me 1,000 rubles—that is, about $200 US dollars (on the black market). It was a fine gift, but not enough to spoil me. But now, because of the *official* exchange rate, every member of the Soviet team had about the equivalent of US $848.00 when we got off the plane! Now *that* was money!

In Budapest, I was stunned at the quantity of goods and the bright colors of the labels. I had never seen such a rainbow of stuff. I went nuts, buying my parents silly things like coffee (for Mom) and cigarettes (for Dad) that were scarce luxury good back home.

I saw and ate my first kiwi fruit there. I saw some team-mates eating some, and I bought one. You couldn't get a fruit like that in the USSR. I was having a great time.

Still, as a fencer, I was a little bit nervous. True, I was used to thinking of myself as a medal contender. And everybody knew that Soviet fencers were good, so that even if I was a new fencer, people would respect me. On the other hand, I was in a new world. The Western fencers wouldn't know me at all. I would have to fight to earn their respect.

In addition, this was the first year we had to use the new Maraging steel blades. It was a safety requirement introduced after Smirnov's death—the new steel was stronger and less likely to break off in a sharp spike. I was unfamiliar with the blades, which were hard to come by at first. I had to borrow some for the tournament. The Maraging blades were heavier than what I was used to fencing with, and the balance was different. At the beginning of the day, I could deal with this, but later on, my fingers became too tired to control my point. I was missing the target more often than I usually did.

I came up out of the pools in reasonable position. In DE's, I beat one Frenchmen, then lost to another Frenchman and the East German Uwe Roemer, taking 23rd place.

I watched Alessandro Puccini of Italy beat Stephan Mie of France in the final. I caught myself thinking that these guys from the West were much too good for me.

Then I realized that the East Germans Ulbrich and Müller had been in the final eight. I couldn't figure out the contradiction: I didn't think I was ready for the final, but I saw two guys there that I had beaten a few months ago in Kiev!

Shopping after the tournament made me feel better. I bought a lot of things that I couldn't have bought in Kiev. I could look different, cooler, than anyone back home.

But now I started thinking.

I saw that the Hungarians lived better than we did, but one thought was still pulsing in my brain: we are the best—we are the Soviets!

Hungary itself was supposedly a Socialist country, and they were much better off than we were. In fact, in the USSR, we were worse off than any Socialist country except Romania.

We flew back to Moscow, and a day later, I returned to Kiev by train. I saw that the streets in Kiev were dirtier, that the restaurants had worse service, that people dressed worse and less colorfully. Suddenly, I was looking at the world with slightly different eyes.

Trying for the World Juniors: Part I

At the beginning of February 1988, I fenced in that year's second USSR Junior Championship. This would decide whether I would be on the Soviet team at the Junior World Championships...or be home in Kiev, reading about it in the sports papers.

I had to satisfy a requirement at the University: a cross-country skiing test. I took a day off near the end of January and went skiing at the far end of Kiev., in the biting cold (-16⁰ Celsius, or 3⁰ Fahrenheit). It was just a week before the tournament. Normally, I would never have gone skiing so close to an important competition, especially in such cold weather. But I had to pass that test!

On February 2, I flew to Tbilisi, the capital of the Georgian SSR. The flight was delayed for ten hours, so I got to bed at 3:30 a.m. on the day of the tournament. I had to fence with only four hours of sleep. I was expecting to fence for Army, like the year before, and was surprised to find that I didn't have to sleep in a barracks. But this time, I was listed as a Dinamo fencer. Weird!

Maybe the lack of sleep did me good, or maybe it was

the skiing the week before. I lost only two bouts in three rounds of pools, made it all the way to the semifinals, where I lost to Oleg Chernyshov 10 – 8, but took bronze by beating Zhitnikov from Moscow, 10 – 2 in the consolation bout.

The exact placing didn't matter to me. I had confirmed my steady results throughout the season and earned a place on the final squad from which the coaches would select the Soviet Team for the Junior World Championships, in South Bend, Indiana, USA!

I was in … except for six more weeks of tryouts …

A Lesson That Stayed With Me

On February 4, 1988, in the aftermath of the tournament, I found a little brochure containing the advice of an American coach and scientist, whose name, unfortunately, I didn't record. Perhaps someone reading this book will recognize the author, even though it's been translated from English to Russian and back again. If you do, let me know, because I owe this man a debt of thanks. His recipe gave me extra strength and motivation for years, and now I pass it on. It appears on the next page:

This recipe, I think, is applicable for every athlete.

Recipe for Sucess

1) Always be self-confident, but don't be arrogant.
2) Always help your opponent; he might become your friend.
3) Learn, learn, learn!
4) Ask any athlete you meet about his techniques and training methods.
5) Compete as often as you can: you need the experience.
6) Don't even think about second place—you came to win!
7) Stay determined, no matter what the conditions, equipment, form, or circumstances of the competition.
8) Always take responsibility for your results. Analyze your mistakes more than your successes.
9) Control your emotions in competition; they can destroy your coordination and wreck your rhythm
10) Stay self-critical, objective, and open.
11) Trust your trainer and share your current problems with him so that you can resolve your difficulties.
12) Study the **physiology** of training and the **psychology** of opponents. *Don't be afraid to experiment!*
13) When it seems that nothing can help you, ask a good athlete for help.
14) Choose a goal and aim for it, if you believe that it is a possible goal.
15) For a person who believes, *there are no limits!*

Trying for the World Juniors: Part II

After a quick return to Kiev, I flew to Leningrad for a camp with the Soviet senior team. It was a great experience, but my main memory of this camp is that I met Aleksandr Romankov, from Byelorussia, one of the very greatest fencers that the USSR ever produced—in my opinion, one of the greatest fencers ever. He was sixteen years older than I was, a five-time individual world champion. If someone is named Aleksandr, we call him Sasha, but there was no way I could call Romankov by that nickname. The age difference and the awe I felt in his presence made me address him formally at all times.

Only two years later, after we had been teammates on the senior team, did I dare to call him Sasha or use the familiar "thou" instead of the formal "you."

The 12th and 13th of February, I fenced in a strong senior international competition in Leningrad. My 22nd place finish was solid, but this time I wasn't at all satisfied. I felt I could have done better.

Then it was on to Podolsk for the last camp before the Junior Worlds. This was where the final selection would be made. I felt confident because my junior point standing was high. It was very unpleasant to be "on the bubble" in the standings—third for the juniors, fourth or fifth for the seniors. Then the coaches could decide your fate and pick someone with fewer points whom they thought was in better shape or had higher potential. Sometimes it was a purely political decision. It's hard on the guy who is ahead on points, but I agreed in principle.

Podolsk is a dreary little industrial city south of Moscow. As far as I know, its claim to fame is that it has a sports center, located in a former great estate, where the Soviet team used to train before the Junior Worlds … always in February or March, always in the cold and snow.

Did I say "the last camp?" Actually, Podolsk consisted of *two* two-week camps, with a week's break between them.

In the first camp, we didn't do much fencing, but a lot of cross-training. We played table tennis, basketball, soccer (in the snow), and we skied. This was another welcome break and a chance to bond with my teammates.

I didn't have a steady coach on the junior team yet. I took one lesson from Markarian, the man who coached my constant rival (and future buddy) Gagik Oganesian. Two days later, I took a lesson from Mikhail Zolotariov, and something clicked from the first touch.

Mikhail was a strongly built Russian with a slight stammer and a fun-loving disposition. People liked him at once, and so did I. I trained with him for a little over a year—until the summer of 1989—and he gave me a lot, especially what I would call a touch of the Russian style: harder on the blade and using flicks (more on this later).

Our relationship became special, as if he had been my older brother. He liked rock and heavy metal music. There were mornings, especially after a party, when he didn't want to give me a lesson. He'd roll over in bed and say, "Do some footwork and fence a little." But I would wake him up and drag him to the fencing room.

We invented a game that we called "billi-hands." As the name implies we used our hands instead of a cue, and we only used one object ball. For a while, the game actually became popular among the junior foilists.

Mikhail Zolotariov was a lot of fun to be around, and I learned a lot from him in the short time we worked together. Even now, many years later, some Russian coaches refer to him as my trainer.

The Flick

As I said, Zolotariov was the first coach to teach me the flick. People always ask me about the flick because it's

> The flick is much less reliable than the thrust.

such a controversial move—some say that it has ruined foil by turning it into sabre; others feel that it is the greatest invention since the wheel.

It was a relatively new move in the late 1980's, produced by a combination of more flexible blades and faster fencing. Not many fencers used it then.

I had learned a strictly classical style from my father, who of course had learned to fence without flicks because they hadn't been invented yet. Besides, I fenced with a French grip for the first four years of my career, and you can't flick very well with a French grip because the handle gets in the way. Anyway, my wrist wasn't strong enough at that age.

Before the flick, fencers had been using a closely related move, the coupé or "cut-over," where you change from one side of your opponent's blade to the other by bringing your wrist back and passing your blade over your opponent's blade and point. This is tactically a logical move, even though it is a slower way of changing sides (engagements) than passing your blade *under* your opponent's blade (disengaging): in order to disengage, you have to *guess* whether your opponent will attempt to make a direct parry or a circular parry. If you guess wrong, your opponent meets your blade in mid-disengage and you are in trouble. So you throw in the coupé, where, since your blade is back, you clear your opponent's normal parry altogether. Of course, you have to time it right. And you can't coupé all the time, or your opponent will catch on and use a parry designed to block the coupé.

Essentially, the flick evolved from the coupé. The coupé finishes the same as a classical touch: the point moves forward to the target and remains on it. The flick is different.

As fencing became faster and more dynamic over the years (like life itself), and as steel became more flexible without losing strength, the flick became possible.

It's faster than the coupé, and because the point doesn't stay on the target, it's easier to get back and parry the opponent's riposte. So the flick suits the modern game perfectly. It's true that it would never have been used in a duel a century ago, but sport evolves.

> The problem with the flick is the way the referees call it. Some fencers come forward with their weapon arm "in their back pocket." That's a preparation, not an attack.

Mikhail Zolotariov taught the flick for only one action: circle-six (counter-six) parry—riposte with a flick to the shoulder. Later, I had a German friend, Thomas Endres, who had a whole arsenal of flicks. I didn't copy his actions (I couldn't have, being from a classical Soviet school), but I liked to watch him and learned new possibilities from him. As you'll see, I started using flicks a lot only in my very last competition as a junior.

In my opinion, the problem with the flick is not the action itself, but the way the referees too often call it. We see fencers advancing with their weapon arm behind their head or "in their back pocket." This is a preparation, not an attack; and if the opponent attacks while the fencer is strolling forward with his arm back, it's an attack on preparation and the fencer is touched—or should be. But too many referees are calling the attack in favor of anyone who is simply coming forward. So the play of the blades is gone, and fencing starts to look like track and field.

How did we get to this sorry state of affairs? The referees were under pressure from the strong fencing countries. They gave in, and then the flick became a fashion.

I used to fence this way myself, because it worked—the referees would give me the touch, and the flick gave me an advantage over the older fencers. In other words, I was fencing with the market. But over time, as more and more fencers rushed to use the flick, the market became glutted and the novelty was gone. It became clear to me: no one-dimensional game can be successful for long.

I have always tried to be flexible in my style, so I could vary the proportion of flicks to thrusts. Over time, I returned increasingly to the classical style. At the end of my career, only 10% of my attacks used flicks. I had "gone back to the future," to my classical roots.

In my opinion, even though the flick is spectacular (and beautiful in slow motion), it is much less reliable than the thrust. A flick travels along a curve, so you will miss if you have misjudged the distance at first or if your opponent closes the distance on you. If you thrust, your point travels along a straight line, so it is easy to stretch your extension or your lunge in order to lengthen your attack, or else to bend your arm in order to shorten it.

As I write this, the International Fencing Federation (FIE) is proposing experimental rule changes, to be tested in Junior World Cups after the 2004 Olympics. They are designed to sharply reduce the number of flicks by increasing the force necessary to score a touch and increasing the length of time the point must remain on the target. I am thoroughly in favor of this idea.

Of course, this won't stop the game from evolving. New techniques will emerge that take maximum advantage of the new rules. And I am in favor of that, too.

My advice is simple: *learn the classical style and keep working on your technique.* When the moment comes to add a new technique, you will have a basis for it.

> Learn the classical style and keep working on your technique! When the time comes for a new technique, you'll have a basis for it.

Trying for the World Juniors: Part III

But I digress again. I was in Podolsk, in midwinter 1988, learning the flick riposte (and refining my classical technique) with Mikhail Zolotariov, while trying to make the final cut for the World Junior Team.

The worst training session was the one at 7:30 in the morning. We would line up in the darkness and freezing cold, feeling like zombies, too cold even to talk to each other. We'd thaw out during breakfast.

The first week's camp had made me think that I was getting stronger. But of course, I overtrained and caught a bad cold. If you look back at my story, you will see the signs that I was constantly on the edge of overtraining. This mistake followed me for years.

Mother Nature didn't endow me with great strength or great endurance. I had to walk a tightrope. I needed to train very hard to be fit, but if I overdid it, I'd arrive at a tournament only half-alive.

Overtraining is unfortunately all too common among athletes. You have trouble sleeping. You blow up over simple things. Your mouth is dry. It gets harder and harder to drag yourself to practice. The psychological result can be burnout, or loss of motivation and satisfaction. The physical result, as in my case, is injury and illness.

Coaches have to plan daily, weekly, and monthly training cycles for athletes. For example, the week of cross-training in Podolsk, followed by a week of rest before the season climaxed with the final selection the Junior World Championships—that was an example of cyclical planning. Unfortunately, training cycles have to be individualized. That means that the coach has to be asking questions of his fencer, and the fencer needs to talk honestly with his coach. You have to know when to ease up. I'm not talking about being lazy; I'm talking about being professional.

> Coaches have to plan individualized training cycles with their athletes. That means the fencer has to talk honestly with the coach.

The second week of the camp was mostly taken up by training competitions. Take the second day after our arrival. In the morning we had pools, two rounds of pools of eight. That made fourteen five-touch bouts (I went 11 – 3). In the afternoon we did two DE finals of eight (I took third and first). Overall, I took second for the day and felt satisfied. The next day, we each had seven ten-touch bouts (I won four and lost three, all by identical scores of 10 – 9 that showed how intense the competition was.) The third day was a day off, so I did 5 km. of cross-country skiing—to relax! The next morning, eight five-touch bouts and five ten-touch bouts.

South Bend, 1988

On March 17, the coaches finally met to make the final decision on the men's foil team for the Junior Worlds. They picked Gagik Oganesian, Oleg Chernyshov … and me! The first thing I did was call my dad with the great news.

I should introduce these guys—teammates, rivals, friends.

Gagik Oganesian is a lefty with a nice smile. He's from Armenia. Like a lot of guys from the mountainous Caucasus, he was a totally sweet person… with a short fuse that kept him one step away from exploding with anger.

Oleg Chernyshov is another lefty from the Caucasus— this time, from Georgia. He had an injury to his right hand so that he couldn't use it, but that didn't impede his fencing in the least. He was my main rival at this time, winning "my" titles again and again in the top junior and cadet tournaments.

A few days before the competition, we were issued our first national-level equipment. I got my first Kevlar uniform, my first Adidas fencing shoes, my first Maraging blades. There was hardly time to fit my handles to the new blades. That led to trouble later on.

We Soviets were proud, but poor. We couldn't afford to eat out in the US. All of us fencers would bring canned food from the USSR to save some pocket money, so that we could buy something with our *forbidden* hard currency. (We got about US $20.00 a day in spending money, but that was all the hard currency we were allowed to have.)

Soviet citizens were forbidden to possess hard currencies. It was a serious economic crime. Naturally, everyone had a secret stash, acquired who knows how.

Before we left for the Junior Worlds South Bend, Grigori Kriss, (the chief of fencing at my home club, Dinamo, and an Olympic epee champion) came up to me.

"Listen," he said, "Don't starve yourself. You'll only do yourself harm. Get yourself one decent meal before you fence." And he slipped me 40 DM (about $24 US at the time).

In those days, even Soviet citizens had to go through customs before leaving the USSR. An officer stopped me. I was strip-searched. They found the 40 DM. I was now a "criminal."

Thank God, it was the era of glasnost (openness) and perestroika (restructuring), when Mikhail Gorbachev was in the middle of his doomed effort to make the USSR into an open, modern country without giving up Communism. I wasn't arrested, but for the rest of the trip, the official bureaucrats on the trip kept looking at me as if I had betrayed my country. As you can imagine, it made me very nervous to think what might happen when we got back to the USSR. My teammates tried to calm me down.

"Relax, Sergei," said the epeeist Skorobogatov. "If you win, they'll leave you alone."

Win? That was easy to say!

Had I ever won an international competition overseas, let alone a Junior World Championship?

We got to our hotel in South Bend at 2:00 a.m. after a tiring trip. Our only thoughts were of a shower and a warm bed. But our coaches called a meeting.

At least I wasn't the only one in trouble: several of the fencers also had trouble leaving the USSR: they were carrying too much caviar (to sell for dollars in the US).

Naturally, after that meeting, there was a room check.

Like practically all Soviet fencers, I had brought fencing equipment for sale: we had been issued far more stuff than we needed, and we brought it along to exchange for dollars. I could squeeze electric vests under the bed, but I couldn't make my bundle of blades disappear fast enough—our chief was walking through the door.

He confiscated the blades, and I didn't get them back until the last day. I had to bring them back with me.

It was part of my punishment for having been caught with hard currency.

So I was distinctly on the official list of troublemakers. But it wasn't enough for me! The very next day, Oleg Chernyshov and I went out to buy tape recorders. Such things were unavailable in the Soviet Union, so of course we wanted to have them. It seemed logical to me that I would take the first opportunity. Naturally, I was caught coming back to my room.

"It would be entirely different if you waited until the last day, Golubitsky. You are a Soviet athlete! You should be completely concentrated on your preparation, not thinking about luxuries! You are a troublemaker!"

…if you consider that what I was doing was trouble …

In my journal, I wrote, "I have no fear." But I was scared to death. Only tournament experience will get you over this.

There's a fencing part of this story, too.

The day before the men's foil competition, I wrote in my Journal:

"I feel good. I have no fear."

But on the morning of the competition, I was dying of fear! My food seemed tasteless—I could barely choke it down. I had to force myself to eat.

I was always a bit nervous before competitions. *Not*

72

being nervous isn't a good sign either. Being a little nervous (not scared to death) gives you a little adrenaline and makes you more alert.

But this time I was scared to death. The only way to get over this is tournament experience.

Puccini, the winner of my first international competition in Hungary, was in my first round pool. He beat me 5 – 4, but I won the rest of my bouts. In the second round, I went 2 – 2, losing to Elvis Gregory, the future Cuban great, and Marco Widmer of Switzerland. I went 3 – 1 in a strong third round, losing to Lee of South Korea and beating the rest (including a revenge victory against Gregory).

Every win, every touch in the pools counts toward seeding in direct elimination. So you fence for every touch so that in DE, you don't have to get the strongest opponents first. But the luck of the draw doesn't work that way: sometimes the strongest fencers lose just enough touches so that you have to fence them early. I got just about the hardest draw possible.

My first opponent was Alexander Koch, the top German fencer. I had never fenced him, though I had seen him in the finals in Budapest. (He would be *senior* world champion a year later.)

It wasn't just a defeat for me. It was a complete humiliation; he was all over me—the bout was over, 10 – 2, in a matter of seconds.

Now I was in the losers' bracket, with my back against the wall. The next bout was against the top *French* fencer.

Again, I had only seen him in Budapest—taking second place! For some reason, I beat him relatively easily, 10 – 4. But during this easy win, I broke a blade … and then the tip of my next foil cracked… and wait a minute! I only had three foils. I finished the bout with my last weapon.

The problem was that I use a special handle of my own design, and I only had two of them … on the weapons that were broken. And I didn't have time to change grips!

(Now my sponsor, Leon Paul, is busy producing my grip, for both right-handers and left-handers. It's called the Golubitsky Pro grip! More about them later on.)

I was called to face Thomas Endres of West Germany. And my only foil had a grip I couldn't stand—ironically, a German grip. Under the circumstances, I didn't fence badly, but I was behind for the whole bout and lost 10 – 8.

It gave me a little comfort when Koch took first, Endres took second, and Puccini took third.

From my Journal:

After the competition, there was a team meeting. A storm of criticism rained down on the heads of the foil fencers, especially on me. I felt that I was less than zero as a fencer.

A few days later, I was reading the main Soviet sports paper. There was an interview with the Chief of the Fencing Team:

"Golubitsky is a pretty talented fencer," he said. "He might have a future as an athlete."

I was stunned.

> I need to vary the rhythm and direction of my footwork. .. I have to learn to concentrate on each touch.

April 10 I was back in Kiev.

From my Journal:

Conclusions from the World Championships:

I have to work more, especially on my footwork. More than that: I have to change my whole footwork style.

Also, I have to learn to concentrate—especially, how to concentrate on each touch.

So all through the following year I was working on my footwork. I had to learn how to vary the direction. I practiced changing direction rapidly—for example, making half-retreat—advance-lunge or double advance—jump back. I had to practice varying my rhythm, too, so that nothing I did would be predictable.

Also, I saw that Alexander Koch of Germany had a special technique for making a double-advance– lunge. After the second advance, his foot wouldn't touch the floor, but immediately kick out into the lunge. I stole that technique from him and used it for a while.

To practice concentration, I did special drills. I'd start a bout behind 3 – 0 and try to catch up, or I'd fence for one touch, like a pentathlete. It was especially important for me to learn to fence for one touch at a time.

The Friendship Tournament

Only a short time after the Junior Worlds, I went to the Friendship Tournament, a junior tournament for the socialist countries that was held in Romania. I was the best Soviet fencer, taking sixth place; I also fenced quite well in the team event, in which we took third.

I was being punished on this trip. I wasn't allowed to exchange my rubles for Romanian lei. Even worse, I had to share a room with the Chief of Delegation, Liashenko, so that he could keep an eye on me.

After being in the United States, I saw clearly that my country was not the first in the world economically. I had learned in school that Marxism-Leninism was the ideal system, while people in the West were suffering miserably under capitalism. Capitalists were exploiting them, sucking their blood, turning them into mindless zombies. The whole system was rotten and doomed to self-destruct in the near future. That's what we were taught.

My first trip abroad, to Hungary, had set a time bomb ticking inside me. On the way back from South Bend, I spent twenty-four hours in Copenhagen, the capital of Denmark. That set the bomb off. I loved that city and realized there that much of what I had been taught wasn't true. Experience was replacing mythology.

The socialist system was supposed to give equal rights to all. Good idea, but ... Hardworking people were earning the same as lazy people; talented people were making the same as idiots. We had no freedom of speech. We had no freedom of travel (when we traveled abroad, we had to walk around in groups—ideally, of five people—so our bosses could be confident that if anyone did something dangerous, like speaking to a foreigner, someone in the group would inform.

The Friendship Tournament ended the junior season and only one big competition remained, the (senior) Championship of the USSR, which was held on June 18, 1988. We trained for it near Kiev. I had to be in two places at once: at training and at the University, where I had exams to take. I managed to split my summer term, passing a couple of tests before the Championships and leaving the rest for afterward. This left me time to train.

The camp was one of the best I can remember. It was well balanced, requiring a lot of fencing, but also a lot of recreational soccer and basketball. I finished in the top three in all the training tournaments and left for Leningrad in good shape.

This championship was coming at a pivotal time for me. I was one of the top juniors of the USSR (not just Ukraine) with one more junior season to go. This had advantages and disadvantages. On the one hand, I was near the top and could reasonably look forward to improving during the coming year. On the other hand, everyone would be fencing me more carefully, and *after* the coming year, I would be a senior, with no realistic chance of breaking into the ranks of the first team.

Fortunately, I wasn't looking that far ahead.

In the first round of the Championships, I had a decent pool. I lost only to Anvar Ibragimov. (Anvar, four years older than me, was a great fencer from the first team—a lefty with very strong legs; who had taken third in the '85 University Games in Kobe, Japan, as well as winning bronze at the Junior World Championships in Leningrad. I had many chances to see him because he fenced for the Army, and I admired his fencing greatly.)

The second round was similar. I had Vladimir Aptsiauri; the rest were beatable. Aptsiauri had been on the team with Vladimir Smirnov when the fatal accident took place. This short, physically powerful man had to carry the sorrow of that tragedy throughout his whole life. I lost to him and to Stepanov—another tall fencer, but not related to my junior rival from Leningrad. With only three losses, I was in the DE's, which would take place the next day.

In the DE's I lost decisively, 10 – 5, to Alexei Shvetsov, a very strong fencer who had been a member of the USSR first team, but for some reason had been kicked off the squad. From then on, it didn't matter what he won in the USSR; they would never allow him to travel abroad.

I won once more in the loser's bracket, beating a Latvian fencer 10 – 9, but then was crushed by my junior rival Ilmar Kuziaev, 10 – 4. I finished twenty-first, while Kuziaev wound up fourth.

Ilmar Kuziaev, a thin, dark-haired fellow, was a painful example for me—he showed me that a junior, my contemporary, could have a high rating among the seniors. I knew—I had to believe—that I, too, could rank much higher. I didn't want to fall behind any juniors!

Actually, though, my twenty-first place was an accurate reflection of my place at that time. I wasn't a threat to the first team … yet.

1989: My Breakthrough Year

Military Service

On my return to Kiev, I plunged back into studying. As you will remember, I had rescheduled some of my exams because of the tournament, and now I had to take them. Also, now that I was eighteen, it was time to serve my country in the armed forces. This was the duty of every healthy young man in the USSR.

I had changed clubs from Army to Dinamo, which was sponsored by the police and the KGB. But the Army was planning to snatch me before Dinamo could get its act together. Bykov, the chief of Army fencing in Ukraine, was still after me. He was in Kiev and could grab me at once, while Dinamo, with its headquarters in Moscow, was still in the dark.

I had to hide out in a friend's room in the dorms at the University. The day after I left, my parents saw soldiers waiting for me. I had already heard stories about Dinamo athletes the Army had grabbed. A couple of soldiers with an officer would show up on the doorstep, and when you opened the door, they would drag you to an Army office, fill out the papers, and induct you. Then you were an Army athlete. I heard one story about how the soldiers had jumped into a pool to snatch one swimmer, and another about two fencers who were snatched in the middle of the night (one of them escaped).

The reason for all this drama is that each organization got points based on the success of its athletes ... and its budget depended on its point standing.

So there I was, taking my exams and heading straight back to my friend's dormitory. No sense in giving anyone a chance to discover my hideout.

The afternoon before, the Dean had promised that I would pass Anatomy after the official end of the semester. The very next morning, I presented myself bright and early at the Dean's office to get his signature.

But the news was bad.

Not only wasn't I going to be able pass Anatomy—he was expelling me from the University!

"Why?" I asked.

"I've received information that you are a draft dodger, a deserter, and a disgrace to the Soviet Union!"

I was shocked and scared. I called my father, and he called Grigori Kriss, the Dinamo fencing chief who had inadvertently gotten me in trouble by slipping me 40 DM before the Junior Worlds. In a matter of minutes both of them were at the Dean's office.

"What's the matter?" Kriss asked.

"Bykov, at the Army Club, called me to say that this young man is a draft dodger."

"It's a lie," said Kriss. "He's going to be recruited by Dinamo in a matter of days."

This satisfied the Dean and all was well. I passed Anatomy and, taking no chances, left Kiev by taxi for our summer cottage. A day or two later, my friend drove me to the railroad station and I boarded a train for Moscow. From there I went back south to Orel with two other newly recruited fencers (one of them, Aleksandr Beketov, was to become Olympic epee champion in the 1996 games in Atlanta). Orel was a big military base that included a sports center for Dinamo's soldiers in all sports and from all parts of the USSR. We made up an athletes' company within the forces of the KGB.

KGB—sounds sinister, doesn't it? Well, we were only athletes. We stayed in barracks with another two companies, with the big difference that they were ordinary soldiers. We had many advantages over them, like TV in our barracks, a later wake-up call, and sports practice instead of marching most of the day. We were special: the future of Soviet sport! ... although in fact, only Beketov, Anatoli Tishenko) and I ever accomplished much. (Anatoli became an Olympic rower; I'd run into him again at the Atlanta and Sydney Olympics, and he was at Athens in 2004.) I used to run into some of the other athletes for a few years, but never heard of them at the top levels.

Only our sergeant and I were from Ukraine; there were a few athletes from Armenia and Georgia; all the rest were Russian. It could be tough, because we Ukrainians were fans of the Dinamo Kiev soccer team, while everyone else rooted for Spartak Moscow. For years, one or the other of these great teams would win the USSR championship. There was a time when our unit was watching the two teams play and I was the only one in the room screaming for Dinamo Kiev (the sergeant didn't dare to shout for Kiev).

When our unit had free time, when all the athletes from all the sports were hanging out in the gym, everyone would fence with me and with each other using sticks. I tried to teach them how to move correctly and how to parry. It was great fun.

We ate in the mess hall with all the other soldiers, eating the same Army food. The bravest of us (including me) would go over the base's fence in the evening and make our way into town where we could enjoy an ice cream or a beer.

One day my commander called me in to tell me that Dinamo was going to transfer me to a Ukrainian unit based in Lvov, in Western Ukraine. I asked him whether I could stay: Orel was the strongest of all the Dinamo athletic units. But I wasn't a top fencer, only a promising junior, and he refused me. A year later, he would beg me to come back. That's getting ahead of the story, though.

I was sworn in, took my uniform and papers, and went straight to Lvov. The bosses there didn't exactly greet me with open arms. They told me that Kiev people like me had the reputation of being arrogant. That was the bad news. Then they told me that I only had to report to the base in Lvov every three months. That was the good news. I would train in camps, fence in tournaments, and show up in Lvov every so often.

The soldiers in Lvov were "grandfathers:" veterans of the service who were close to finishing their terms. I was a new recruit. I was happy that they let me alone. I didn't have to do much: just show up, report my tournament results, spend a few uncomfortable nights in barracks, and go home. A year later, all this would be different. They would tell me I didn't even have to show up, just stay in Kiev and train. Again, that's getting ahead of the story.

What a difference a year would make!

But in the meantime, with all of this soldiering, I hadn't trained for the whole month of July I was completely unprepared for my last season as a junior … my dream season.

1988—1989

In early August 1988, I was summoned up north to Tallinn, Estonia, an old trading port on the Baltic Sea, for a two-week camp before the USSR Team Cup. I started out feeling great. I was hungry for fencing after my layoff. But as usual, I overtrained so much that by the second session I had a pounding headache. The top fencers in the Soviet Union were there, and of course we had a few training competitions.

The first day was a marathon round-robin individual competition of twenty-one. We fenced morning and evening sessions. At the end, I took a respectable third place with a 14 – 6 record, beating two fencers who had always defeated me in the past, Andrey Kliushin and Igor Vainberg. After a month of Army service, I felt good about the result.

The next day, they divided us into teams. Mine consisted of the great Romankov (what an honor!); Dmitri Shevchenko, two years older than I was; my junior rival Ilmar Kuziaev, and Valery Novikov. The veterans on all the teams had the idea of "making it interesting:" everyone kicked in three rubles. This small sum made the competition quite intense. I was tired after the individual competition, but managed not to disgrace myself. My teammates carried me to a win in this "commercial" competition.

The rest of the camp was a nightmare. I think I lost to everyone. I have only one positive memory: I won a bout with Romankov, 5 – 4.

The Team Cup took place in Tallinn right after the camp. I had a fever and food poisoning, spending the night before the tournament in the bathroom, puking. My team did quite badly, taking eighth place.

The following week, I had a Ukrainian camp in the Carpathian Mountains of Western Ukraine. My dad was in charge. We did a lot of running in the mountains and a lot of footwork. On the days we didn't have a third session, we would go into the mountains to gather mushrooms or berries. It was a perfect camp, after which I almost felt ready for the season.

After a week off, I went to Alushta in the Crimea to train with the USSR Junior Team. This was during the Olympics in Seoul. Our Soviet men's foil team created a miracle there: Aleksandr Romankov, Boris Koretski, Vladimir Aptsiauri, Anvar Ibragimov, and Ilgar Mamedov won the gold, defeating West Germany decisively, 9 – 5. They hadn't done that since 1964, more than twenty years. (Romankov took individual bronze as well.) I was immensely proud of them.

On the other hand, their success created an obstacle for those of us who had the ambition of being on the first team. How could I dream of breaking into the top five? There were talented veterans far ahead of me in the pecking order. All that was left for me was to train as hard as I could, and I did.

My father kept telling me that it wasn't enough to be the first in the fencing room and the last to leave. I had to outdo my rivals. I started coming a half-hour before anyone else for morning training. Every morning, I would meet the skeptical stares of my sleepy teammates as they sleepily lined up and I jogged sweatily into place next to them.

The emphasis of the camp was on improving our physical abilities. We worked on running, jumping, strength, stamina, and many different tests. In this department, I placed first overall, not just among foil fencers, but on the team as a whole. Not bad for someone without great physical strength or endurance at the beginning of his career!

Of course, we fenced, too. I was building confidence. At the last training competition, I won all my bouts by at least five touches!

I felt ready for the season!

My Last Junior Season

The camp had been a preparation for the Kiev Junior International Tournament. This would be my third and last time fencing in this tournament in my home town, which I had won the year before. The field included the best juniors of the USSR, Hungary, Romania, and Bulgaria. Needless to say, I wanted to defend my title and get off to a good start in my last junior year.

I got off to that good start, winning all fifteen bouts in three rounds of pools. Then I ran out of steam. I lost in the DE's, but sneaked through to the final, beating my teammate Oleg Chernyshov 10 – 6 in the semis, but feeling half-dead. I had to face Balint, a tall Romanian left-hander who would defect to West Germany the following year. (I heard later that he had dropped out of fencing.)

I could do nothing against him. I wanted badly to win, but wanting isn't enough. My legs wouldn't move. My blade would catch the air instead of Balint's blade. I was crushed, 10 – 5.

The next day was the team event. I fenced for the USSR, and we won first place.

Looking back, I can see some of the mistakes I was making in my preparation. I never knew when to rest and relax instead of training harder and harder. I never paid attention to headaches, flue, nosebleed, or sprains. I would take an aspirin, put on some sports cream, and go on. I think sometimes that if I had trained less, I might have achieved more in my fencing career.

After two intensive training camps and three days of tournament, I went to Sukhumi, in Georgia, for another sixteen-day camp. When we got there, I went with a teammate to the shore of the Black Sea. It was in the middle of a storm. I had never seen such high waves, but for some reason, we decided to take a swim.

Our first problem wasn't so serious: we couldn't get into the water because the waves were pushing us back. The next problem was more serious: we couldn't get *out* of the water for the same reason! We finally crawled out, spitting out seawater and scarcely breathing. We could have drowned.

At the camp , it was the same old story. Three days into training, I had a headache but kept going. Then I sprained my ankle playing soccer. After seven days of three-a-day sessions, we had a day off. I ran 10K in 47:00. After that, I felt worse every day. By the end of camp, I had the flu.

I still hadn't recovered by the time of the all-Soviet competition in the ancient caravan city of Tashkent, Uzbekistan. It was the second qualifying competition—the first had been Kiev. I was OK in the first round of pools, but in the second, I started to die. Once again, I managed to crawl into the final eight, losing to Pavlovich, who would later win team gold in Atlanta. The next day, the Ukrainian team managed third place. I returned to Kiev barely alive. Even my father took it easy on me.

Then we received an unexpected invitation. The USSR junior team was going to France for a Junior World Cup. I would be flying, with three other foilists and a coach, to Aix-en-Provence at the expense of the French organizers. This would be my second Junior World Cup, almost a year after Budapest, my first.

Naturally, we had to prepare with another camp, this one in Moscow. This wasn't a large-scale formal camp: because the squad was so small, we could stay at Dinamo's hotel and train at the Dinamo fencing room, located under the stands of the Dinamo stadium. The camp wasn't hard at all: it felt like training back in Kiev, except that I was taking lessons from Zolotariov instead of my father. I even had some free time. I went to a concert and to the wedding of two of Zolotariov's students, Inna Rodionova and Anton Antokhin.

There was an informal, home-like atmosphere that relaxed me. I felt really good as we headed to France. The atmosphere improved even more on the flight as we ate caviar.

This was my first visit to France. It was really an unfair comparison: winter in frozen Moscow versus winter in warm Provence! I also appreciated the delicious food and the friendly, smiling people.

Maybe all the relaxation had an effect on my fencing. I won twelve of fifteen bouts in three rounds of pools and was seeded tenth in the direct elimination. I beat an Italian,

Fabio Di Russo (later my friend) but then lost to Becker of West Germany 10 – 5 and had to make my way through the losers' bracket. After two wins, I found myself in a revenge match with Becker, and beat him 10 – 5 to make my first World Cup final.

In the round of eight, I met Alex Koch. The memory of his win over me in South Bend at the Junior Worlds still rankled. The bout was fairly even, but in the end, the victory was again his, by a score of 10 – 8.

My teammates were also successful: Pavlovich made the top eight along with me, while Ilmar Kuziaev made the top four. In other words, I was doing well, but not gaining any ground!

I spoke a little English and was never afraid to use it, even though it was far from perfect. I was talking to some of the Italians and they invited me to a party in their room. I took Kuziaev with me, and of course a bottle of vodka. The room was full of Italians and Germans. I was eager to talk with foreign fencers, to make friends. I was keen to learn how they lived and trained and what they thought of us Soviets and the rest of the "socialist" countries. I wanted to compare "them" with "us."

> I spoke a little English and was never afraid to use it. I was eager to talk with foreign fencers, to make friends.

We sat around, drinking and talking about nothing much. Ilmar didn't talk at all, because he didn't know any of the languages being spoken. Gradually, I became aware that the rest of the world was a little afraid of the "Russian bear," whom they pictured as a hulking brute like Ivan Drago, as played by Dolph Lundgren in the "Rocky" movies (we'll meet Dolph/Ivan later). As for me, I didn't have a stereotype for Westerners. I was just curious about them. I didn't mind the differences—after all, I was different from the rest of the Soviets. People have different temperaments and different characters, but all of us are made from the same material.

It was a great evening. I was happy with my fencing and the results of the tournament. And I was happy that I could make some friends. Over the years, I have made many more.

The World Cup had taken place on December 3. Just three days later my junior teammates and I were at the Olympic training center outside Minsk, the capital of Belorussia, for another monster two-week camp alongside the national team. We were preparing for the USSR Tournament of the Strongest.

Those of us who were just back from France had quite a few goodies with us. Ilmar Kuziaev had won a new track suit. Others of us had bought sweaters, T-shirts, little travel cases. They were quite a hit at the camp. One very strong fencer asked me whether I had anything else—to sell.

"No," I said.

"Then why did you go?" he asked, scornfully.

"To fence," I answered.

He looked at me as if I had two heads: "Yeah, right!"

I realized that for some athletes, just going abroad was more important than winning, and bringing stuff back for resale was most important of all.

I didn't agree with that.

As usual, by the end of the first day, I had a nosebleed. The whole first week was pretty much a washout. I started arguing with my coach, Zolotariov, on the slightest pretext. I lost to practically everyone. Toward the middle of the camp, however, I started to recover. I should say that it was so cold at that camp that we didn't train in the early morning. We used to luxuriate in our beds until 8:30, soaking up every moment of rest!

As I recovered, I began to enjoy working with Zolotariov a little better. He had traveled with us to Aix-en-Provence and observed both my own fencing and that of my opponents, so he could give me specific actions to use against each of the world's top juniors.

It really worked for me to train at home with my father and at the camps with Zolushka, as we called Zolotariov (it means Cinderella in Russian). Zolushka worked on my coordination and taught specific actions, while my father would work on perfecting my technique and balance. Over time, I combined these two aspects, slowly but surely becoming more complete as a fencer.

The camp continued. I took fourth place in a training tournament of twenty three fencers, with wins over Koretski and Aptsiauri of the Olympic Gold Medal Team, and Slava Grigoriev, a future two-time Olympian. I was elated. The next day, in another training competition, I took third. I was so happy with my fencing and results that I didn't feel any fatigue: *Winners don't get tired! Winners don't feel the pain!* I felt as if I was "the one!"

This euphoria can give you extra energy for a while, keeping the pain and weariness at bay, but you can't fool your body for too long.

The camp ended and the Tournament of the Strongest was at hand. It was my birthday, December 20, 1988. I felt really good, almost perfect. The first day, out of ten bouts … I won … *three!* It was a disaster. The next day, it was no better: I went out in the first round, taking thirty-second place overall.

I had felt terrible and done well.

The way you feel before the competition has no bearing on the result!

I learned an important lesson from this failure. I had felt great and done terribly; at other times, I had felt terrible and done well.

The way you feel before the competition has no bearing on the result!

And again, I was keenly aware how far I was from the top of Soviet fencing.

I came back from the Tournament of the Strongest in

a really bad mood. But I was also determined to make my bad experience work for me. I would turn it into a motivating force that would push me forward and me turn it around.

The negative result would help me to create a positive outcome!

> I was determined to make my bad experience work for me. The negative result would help me create a positive outcome!

1989: Breakthrough!

I came back to Kiev tired, so I cut back on my training. On New Year's Eve, I had a chance to relax with family and friends. Then I had to start thinking about preparing for my last Junior World Cup.

At that time, there weren't as many Junior World Cups as there are now, so each one was more important, and fencers from all over the world would attend. The biggest of all was Budapest. A good result in Budapest would win the respect of the other fencers, which was pleasant. More importantly, it would win you the all-important respect of the referees at the Junior Worlds—which might be essential.

I got off to a great start, to put it mildly, losing just one bout (5 – 4) in three rounds of pools. It was the same in direct elimination. I cruised through the table, 10 – 5, 10 – 7, 10 – 3, making my second consecutive table of eight. In the semifinal, I ran into my friend Fabio Di Russo, who took revenge for my win over him in Aix-en-Provence. It was a close, hard-fought bout, I lost 12 – 10 (you had to win by two at that time). In the consolation bout, I was dead physically, and could do nothing at all with my opponent, the slender, outgoing French right-hander Christophe Bel. He beat me up, 10 – 4, to leave me in fourth place.

But this result gave me a second wind for the rest of the season. It would become the season of my dreams.

I joined the Ukrainian junior squad in the small city of Belaia Zerkov, about seventy-five miles south of Kiev. We trained for a week and headed for the next Soviet Tournament of the Strongest.

At this event, I faced an interesting set of opponents in the third round of pools. The first was Andrey Kliushin, a smart left-hander from Leningrad who later became my friend and preferred roommate when I made it to the Soviet first team. He was already on that first team, as were two more of my next opponents, Ilgar Mamedov and Boris Koretski, members of the Gold Medal Olympic squad. Besides these titans, there was Andrey Pavlov (another student of Zolotariov from that first Dinamo camp), another youngster, and me.

The pool system isn't perfect, as this round illustrated. If you ran into a group of people who had made a deal among themselves to throw bouts to each other, you would have to beat all of them to avoid elimination. Big problem: I wasn't strong enough to beat all of the senior squad members, but didn't know them well enough to get into their little deal. Later we'd be friends, but not yet!

In the old pool system, it was easy for people to throw bouts to each other.

Kliushin lost to me and another youngster. It was a major error on his part. Now he would need wins over Mamedov and Koretski. He wasn't going to get them. Mamedov, Koretski, and Pavlov fenced a "happy round" among themselves. The deal was that each of them would win one and lose one. I tried to make a side deal with Mamedov by asking for four touches. I hoped that if I beat Pavlov, I'd go up with a better indicator (difference between touches scored and touches received). It was no go. So I lost badly to Mamedov, and then, on top of it, I lost the important bout to Pavlov. That dropped me into the lowest final, the "C" final.

(Kliushin tried to complain about the "fix" to Perekalski, his coach on the national team, but it was too late. He was out, too.)

Fencing in the "C" final, I wound up fifteenth overall.

Fifteenth! After a fixed pool, I'd finished fifteenth—my second best result ever in senior competition! That motivated me for my last Soviet Junior Championship, which would take place in ten days.

I fenced well in this tournament. Mom and Dad were with me, it was fun to watch my two coaches interacting, and Zolotariov could always find a way to make everyone laugh.

The only thing that marred the competition was being ahead of Oleg Chernyshov 7 – 4 in the climactic competition, but then blowing the lead and losing. I was the top Soviet junior by point standings! I had a higher world ranking! I had no right to lose!

I resolved to be even hungrier for the Friendship Tournament in Godollo, Hungary, where I would face all the top juniors from the East Bloc. In addition to the individual competition, I would be on the team with Oleg Chernyshov, Smirnov (the "other" Smirnov, that is), Pavlovich, and Sitkin.

The Junior Friendship Tournament, 1989

In the first round of pools, I won all my bouts, but was surprised to see the face of my teammate Oleg Chernyshov as my first opponent in the second round pool. We made a deal to fence to 4 – 4 and then fight for the last touch. I won this and all my other bouts in this pool.

As was becoming almost a habit with me, I made it into the final of eight … by way of the losers' bracket, thanks to a loss to an East German named Langner. I was very tired, but fortunately had some time to recover before the final was fenced.

All I can say about what came next is that *something happened to me!* I felt confident, and my style improved. In the quarter- and semifinals, I won 10 – 5 and 10 – 4, almost without breaking a sweat. In the final, I faced Langner, who had beaten me earlier, but once again, no problem. I got a very, very solid revenge, 10 – 3 (!).

To make things even sweeter, my teammates all finished in the top sixteen—and the team won the gold medal.

And I was certain that I had nailed down my plane ticket for Athens and the Junior World Championships.

As if I was being punished for success, I was sent immediately to cold, dark Podolsk, in a training center far from civilization, for two weeks of camps. Fence, eat, fence, eat, fence, eat, sleep, fence … with maybe time for a shower in between. Well, there was a movie theatre, too.

In the middle of the second camp, they held a senior tournament. It was a qualifier for the Soviet senior team, but the result didn't matter much to me because I was on the Junior World Team, which was all that I cared about. As a result, I was pretty relaxed and fenced that way. I made it to the final of eight, where all the "big guys" were waiting for me.

Maybe the "big guys" weren't taking me seriously yet, or maybe I was just relaxed while they were tight, but I beat Kliushin 10 – 7 in the quarters, Grigoriev 10 – 7 in the semis, and lost to Koretski 10 – 7 in the final (my diary reads "bad refereeing") to take silver.

I was so busy thinking about the Junior World Championships that I didn't have time to let this result sink in, which was just as well.

"It might have been a fluke," I would tell myself. I might have just got lucky."

I tried to forget about it and focus on my preparation.

Back in Podolsk, I continued the backbreaking routine of endless sparring.

During a break one day, Oleg Glazov, the head coach of the junior team sat down next to me and asked me a startling question:

"Who do you think should be on the foil team for Athens?"

I was speechless. The head coach was asking *me?* I was in for sure, but only two of the next three could make it. I said that the "old guys" should go: for Kuziaiev and Chernyshov, it would be their last shot at the Junior Worlds; Pavlovich would get two more chances. Oleg asked my reasoning. I explained that two years before, at the Junior World Championships in Sao Paulo, Brazil, a team of three "old guys" had done well: Shevchenko became world champion and the other two were in the top eight. Besides, I said, Pavlovich wasn't clearly better than the other two.

Glazov looked at me and said, "OK." Then he left.

I have no idea whether my words had any influence on the eventual decision, but in the end, Pavlovich had to stay home. I was pleased, though, that somebody, and somebody important at that, had asked my opinion.

We arrived in Athens a few days before the competition and did our best to adjust to the sweltering heat (It was only March!) I couldn't breathe for the first few days, but after a few practices I was feeling more or less OK.

The Junior World Foil Championships began. I got through the first round easily, but the second became a nightmare.

Three of six would go up from our second round pool. Zalichowski, a Polish fencer, asked me for four touches. That was OK with me. I beat him 5 – 4. I won my next two also, but lost unexpectedly to the Australian Young, in a close bout. I had three victories and only one loss, but three other fencers stood at least as well as I did. My touch count in the next bout would decide whether or not I would advance to the next round. I would be fencing Elvis Gregory of Cuba—a tough match.

Mikhail Zolotariov, my coach, studied the score sheet intently. "Sergei," he said gravely, "you need to score at least two touches to be sure of going up"

I froze with shock. I had thought I stood better than that. I went up against Gregory all tensed up. I was lucky to get even one touch against him.

"Well, that's it," I thought. All the training, all the waiting, all the pain—it was all history. I was out in the second round.

Then Zolotariov walked past me. Very calmly, as if nothing had happened, he said, "Get your jacket back on. You made it by one touch. Get ready for the third round."

I got my wings back.

I wasn't even mad at Zolushka for his cruel joke—I would have been through (on indicators) even if I had lost 5 – 0. He wanted to see how I would react to the pressure!

In the third round, I was relaxed and fenced well, but a strange situation developed. Thomas Endres and I had four wins each; we'd both advance to the direct elimination table. Langner of East Germany had two victories. Surprisingly, Elvis Gregory had only one victory, as did Maged Shaker of Egypt. My last bout would be against Shaker, and Gregory would fence the final bout of the pool against Langner.

I went onto the strip relaxed. I was up anyway, and I figured I wasn't going to lose to some random Egyptian, who probably didn't even know how to hold a foil properly! (I didn't ask myself how he got to the third round of the World Championships.) Stuff happens. Before I woke up, I was down 3 – 0.

The Cubans on the sidelines started to go crazy. They insisted that the bout be stopped; then they went to the Directoire Technique (the Bout Committee) and accused me of giving the bout away. The head of the USSR team stalked up to me. "Stop this circus!" he growled. "Fence the way you're supposed to!"

I didn't understand. I *was* fencing—just not very successfully! I didn't know this guy; I had never talked with him; there wasn't any underhanded deal. The bout resumed.

Immediately, I scored a touch and hoped that everyone would relax. But no. It was the only touch I managed.

Now it was Gregory's turn. A few weeks earlier, he'd placed fourth at a "Martini" in Paris, one of the most important events on the *senior* circuit. And now this Golubitsky was playing a dirty trick on him—and we were both from the "Socialist camp" and were supposed to be allies. Under this burden of "betrayal," Gregory lost to Langner, the first big upset of the championships.

It wasn't good at all. I tried to talk to the Cuban coach, but he just muttered something in Spanish. I guessed that it wasn't a compliment.

After that rocky start, Elvis and I became friends later on. He defected after the 2002 World Championships in Lisbon and now lives in Italy.

It's hard to believe now, but wheeling and dealing for bouts and touches was very common under the rules in force at that time. If you were pretty sure of advancing, you could give up a few touches. I really did this in the second round with the Polish fencer—and it almost came back to haunt me! You could even dump a bout (like I *didn't* do with Shaker). Of course, it was absolutely wrong and unfair, but it was the way things were done.

The FIE eventually did the right thing, seeding from one round of pools straight into direct elimination to make this kind of thing almost impossible. You can't dump a bout in direct elimination!

The tournament went on, of course. I got Langner for the third time of the day, beating him 10 – 2. My next opponent, for a place in the top eight was...Alex Koch. It didn't look good. He had beaten me the only two times we had fenced. At the beginning of the bout, he was eating me alive. After what seemed like only a few seconds, I was down 8 – 2.

What happened next I still have no idea. I guess I forgot to be afraid. I started to move better. I thought of things we had been working on in practice. I won the bout 10 – 8, to become the only Soviet in the final of eight.

My first bout in the quarter finals was my friend Thomas Endres. We had met at earlier competitions and hung out together. Thomas was already quite an experienced fencer, having won a silver medal on the German team at the Seoul Olympics. We had a pretty even bout, but eventually he got the better of me, 10 – 8. (In the end, he lost to Ye Chong of China for the gold medal.) My friend Fabio Di Russo took the bronze. I had met him the same way I met Thomas. Maged Shaker was in that final eight, too. I guess he knew how to hold a foil, after all. He's my friend now, and lives in the United States.

After the championships, on the last evening, I went out with some Germans, Italians, and others. The rest of the Soviets stayed in their rooms. I remember that one fencer asked me whether I had another year to go in the junior ranks, and that he screamed with joy when he found out that I was not to be part of his junior future.

But I was disappointed. *I hadn't ended my junior career with a medal.* What now, I asked myself. I was a senior now, along with all the older fencers. Junior results are one thing; it's much tougher as a senior. It's like that song, "You're in the Army now!" You're a senior.

> I hadn't ended my junior career with a medal. What would happen to me as a senior?

Two weeks later, I fenced my last junior tournament in Ukraine, and something happened to my fencing. It was as if another person took over my body. I was invincible. My opponents could hardly touch me. I won 10 – 1 in the quarter finals, 10 – 2 in the semis and 10 – 1 in the final. But it wasn't just the scores. I was more decisive in my bladework; I moved differently; I touched frequently with flicks. Most of the Ukrainians—most of the Soviets, for that matter—still weren't using the flick yet.

It was unreal. After the competition I got drunk. It was my last farewell to my life as a junior.

I went home to Kiev. The next day, the telephone rang. It was Alexandr Perekalski the head coach of the USSR senior team. "Would you like to come and train with us?" he asked.

I felt as if someone had just told me I'd won eighty-three million dollars in the lottery.

Was this a trick question?

What a tough choice…between "Yes!" and "Yes, of course!"

I had Oleg Glazov to thank for this. He was the chief of the junior team. He'd asked Perekalski to include me.

And I had even more good news: my father was invited as well. Great!

Now, for the first time, I was among the stars, not as a talented junior, but as a senior. Romankov, Koretski, Aptsiauri, Kliushin, Mamedov, Shevchenko, Ibragimov, Grigoriev… How could I dream of being their equal?

But now, starting to fence regularly with them, I started to win. We were all human, after all. It was just a training camp, but I began to question whether they were so far ahead of me after all. They looked down at me as just another kid, but I didn't have to pay attention to their skeptical looks.

I was fencing the way I had done in my last junior tournament, using a lot of flicks. It was very new to the established stars. Koretski and Romankov would take me aside and explain to me that the flick was no good: I had chosen the wrong path by fencing this way. I listened politely and continued to do my thing. It was legal, it was effective, and it gave me a needed edge. I was winning some bouts, even against the big guys like Romankov; and when I lost, it wasn't by much. Emotionally, I felt great. Physically, however, I was exhausted.

I guess I forgot to be afraid. I started to use moves I had been practicing and went from being down 6 – 2 to winning 10 – 8.

Then I had to go back and train with the Ukrainian team for the USSR Championship. As a result of fatigue, I sprained my left ankle, but I missed only one session, got the ankle taped, and continued training.

The USSR Championship was held in Raubichi, just outside Minsk, the 900-year-old capital of what is now Belarus. We arrived on May 15, 1989. I wasn't at all nervous—these championships meant nothing to me. I expected nothing, and nothing was expected of me.

After all, it wasn't as if I was going to be picked for the Senior World Championships!

With this relaxed attitude, I emerged from the pools (without having fenced particularly well) and breezed through two bouts in direct elimination, 10 – 4 and 10 – 1. I was one bout from the final of eight! In my path was Ildar Shaimardanov, a silent lefthander from Kazan. He had trained with the national team for years and I had never beaten him, but this time, the victory was mine, 10 – 6. Whoa, I'm in the final!

In the quarterfinals, I met Andrey Kliushin, a very tall, skinny leftie from Leningrad. The bout is etched in my memory. I led 9 – 5. 9 – 5! And once again, I couldn't make the last touch. I stopped making decent actions, hoping, I guess, to get lucky. Andrey, on the other hand, scored six consecutive touches to beat me 11 – 9 and leave me in eighth place.

I almost didn't fence the team event because of exhaustion. But I was happy. I had reached a milestone: the finals of the national championships.

I learned a lesson in my next tournament. The Dinamo team traveled to Potsdam, East Germany, for an East Bloc competition against the best East Germans, Poles, and Cubans. I knew hardly anyone except a few whom I had met in the junior ranks.

By rule, if there are teammates in a pool, they fence each other first. As a result, I was joined in the second round pool by my compatriot, Vainberg. He had an arrogant look on his face before the bout and didn't talk to me much. Too bad. We went out on the strip and within seconds, I had beaten him 5 – 0.

He was furious. Didn't I know—he asked—how teammates are supposed to fence against each other? As a matter of fact, I didn't, so he told me. I was supposed to give him four touches and fence for the last one. OK, but I'm pretty sure that he figured he would beat me easily; that was why he hadn't tried to make the deal with me in advance.

I had to fight for my status on the team, to prove that I was an equal.

That year, the FIE was trying an experiment to speed up its tournaments. I had a fairly high seeding and got two chances to fence for the final: if I won my first, I would go straight in; if I lost, I would get another chance. On top of that, my quadrant of the direct elimination table looked to be the easy one, and that proved to be the case.

I cruised through the quarters and semis, meeting the Cuban Betancourt in the final. I only knew him by name; I'd never fenced him; but I guess I was "in the zone," fencing with no fear. I led throughout the bout and won my first senior tournament ever abroad, 10 – 8. It seemed too good to be true. I was tired but very happy.

Mercifully, the chief of our delegation let me rest for the team event, and the next day we went to East Berlin, where I noted how much richer the East Germans were, and we had a good time eating sausages and drinking the great German beer.

Flight back to Moscow.

Night train to Kiev.

Flight to Sukhumi, down in the Georgian SSR.

Another camp—to prepare us for the "Friendship Tournament" of the socialist countries.

When I arrived there, a few days late, I could see the surprise in Coach Perekalski's eyes when I told him about my result in Potsdam, and I could sense the disbelief in the other senior fencers, even as they congratulated me.

I could read the thought behind their words: "Just lucky!"

We'd see.

The camp was almost restful at first—just one practice a day. I could take in the sun and the sea and absorb their energy. But I remember a little clash with Coach Perekalski. He was in charge of the footwork. Every time I'd lunge, he'd correct me: "Golubitsky, don't hit the ceiling! Golubitsky, you're holding your arm too high. Golubitsky, lower your arm!"

> Coach kept yelling at me to keep my arm down: "Don't hit the ceiling!"
> I kept doing it my way.
> I was dead wrong.
> Now I tell my own students the same thing.

I swear I wasn't doing it on purpose, but the next time I lunged, I raised my arm again.

This time, he sounded irritated. "Kid—arm down!"

You think I managed to do it? Nah.

By this time, everybody on the team was staring at me as if I was a kamikaze. They know Perekalski's temper. I didn't—yet.

I repeated my wrong-armed lunge. He was furious. He threatened to kick me off the team. I was absolutely sure that I was lunging right—not that anyone had ever taught me that way, but I just didn't want to give it up.

Politically, it was very important for me to get on the head coach's good side—but I had my principles and vision, even then—even if I was wrong.

As it happens, I was dead wrong. As a coach now, I find myself saying the same thing as Perekalski, over and over again.

After that, Perekalski had two names for me—"stubborn Ukrainian" and *"kid!"*

I must have been doing something right, though (just not those lunges). At the camp's final tournament, I went 7 – 0. No one touched me more than twice. In high spirits, I headed to Leningrad for the "Friendship Tournament" with the national team.

The night before the tournament, I didn't sleep well. I felt sick and kept coughing. In the morning, I felt dreadful, but I really wanted to fence. When the tournament started, I found that I was fencing with confidence. I looked on it as an important *practice session* for my fencing future—no more and no less.

The first round was fairly easy. In the second round, I had three teammates from the USSR first team—Ildar Shaimardanov, Slava Grigoriev, and Anvar Ibragimov— plus the Hungarian Gatai and the Romanian Busan. Amazingly, I won all my bouts in that pool, l beat Gatai again in the DE's, and faced the East German Jarosch to make the final of eight.

I still remember that in between the referee's commands,

I was joking with Coach Zolotariov. He was cracking up, but trying at the same time to tell me to get serious.

But I didn't care! I was having fun.

And I won, 10 – 7.

It was my eighth consecutive final of the year, and more importantly, my fourth straight as a senior.

In the quarters, I met Jarosch again: 10 – 4. Then Uwe Roemer in the semis: 10 – 6. In the finals—for the third time that day—Gatai.

Just toward the end of the bout, I started to have trouble—because I started thinking about winning the tournament instead of getting the next touch. But I had learned something from all my previous defeats. I refocused myself, forcing myself to concentrate on the right actions and the right tactics.

> I had learned from my defeats: I refocused, forcing myself to concentrate on the right actions and the right tactics.

10 – 8! Victory!—my second championship in a row in international competition.

This is what I wrote in my fencing diary the night after the tournament:

From my Journal:

I'm happy! ... I was really nervous before the final, but got through. WON!!

It seems that there is a <u>chance</u> to be on the team for the World Championships in Denver. I couldn't have dreamed it. I can't believe it.

Time will tell...

1989: Trying to Make the Team

In some countries, you earn your place on a team by objective standards, measured by results. It wasn't that way in the USSR. You were selected after a complex struggle between rival factions.

I already mentioned that the USSR men's foil team had won Olympic Gold in Seoul, Korea in 1988. To make the team for the Senior Worlds, I would have to be very strong. I was lucky that it was a post-Olympic year. Romankov, Shevchenko, Mamedov, and Koretski were certain choices for Denver; they'd already packed their bags. But Aptsiauri had taken the year off, and Ibragimov had let himself relax a little and wasn't in his best shape.

That meant that the fifth position was available. It was true that Coach Perekalski wanted Slava Grigoriev to be number five. But Slava had only one good result so far: a ninth place at the Venice World Cup—not exactly shabby, but not decisive, either. And he was Perekalski's pupil, so the selectors were aware of his possible bias.

I had pluses and minuses, too.

The pluses:
- Some of my results this year had been spectacular.
- I was the youngest, and therefore maybe had the highest potential.

The minuses:
- I was totally inexperienced in Senior World Cup competition, and thus
- Nobody (including me) had any idea how I'd do under real pressure, and
- I wasn't the student of any of the national team

coaches, so
- None of them would go out of his way to fight for me.

At that time, there were three trainers (chief coaches) of the USSR men's foil team. Each of them had a larger or smaller group of fencers.

Coach Perekalski worked with Kliushin, Aptsiauri, and Grigoriev. He'd been the team chief when Smirnov was alive, but later, through some mistake or other, he'd lost his post, only to regain it again after a long exile. During that time, Soviet foil had gone downhill, and only after his return, just ten months before the triumphant Seoul Olympics, had men's foil returned to its glory.

Surely *his* recommendation would count for something! (At this point, I thought about that raised arm and my title of "stubborn Ukrainian," and I shuddered inside.) I had a lot of respect for him, but we didn't know each other.

Ernest Asievski was working with Romankov and Koretski, who were certain to make the team. Mark Midler was working with Shevchenko and Mamedov, also sure to make it, plus Ibragimov, Shaimardanov, and Vainberg—all rivals.

I was lucky that one of the top bosses of the Sport Committee had watched the Leningrad Friendship Tournament that I'd won. He'd fight for me, as would my chiefs at Dinamo.

But it was my coach, "Zolushka" (Mikhail Zolotariov), to whom I owe the debt of gratitude. He really stepped up for me—or rather, stepped down. Zolushka told Perekalski that he'd agree *not to coach me* any more. The decision was painful for both of us. He gave up *his* chance for glory so that I could have mine. Perekalski took me under his wing and became my trainer, taking charge of my preparation. That's how I snatched the coveted fifth spot on the team.

Thanks, Zolushka! I haven't forgotten.

The last camp before Denver was held in Tsakhadzor, Armenia, a resort town 6000 feet up in the mountains with a famous old monastery and, more to the point, a sports complex built in 1960. I shared a luxury *suite* with Romankov—we had a bedroom and a living room, a TV, a refrigerator…and, if we were *very* lucky, a little bit of running water (well, you can't have everything). It ran at most once a day. When it ran, we'd try to collect it in the bathtub. It made for problems with showering, laundry, brushing our teeth…

Oh, and another small problem: the earthquakes. Armenia is on a massive fault line. The year before, a massive earthquake in Armenia had taken the lives of thousands of people. We had to stay alert. And yes, in the middle of one memorable night, the building *did* tremble and heave, and we all ran out. But there was no serious damage, and it only happened once.

We were training at altitude because we'd be fencing in Denver, "The Mile High City." It wasn't a bad idea in principle, but I got nosebleeds and headaches every day.

Also, I was now taking lessons from Perekalski. Anytime you change coaches, there's a period of adjustment—you have to learn a new motion stereotype, develop new kinetic memories. In other words, you are doing even the simplest actions a little differently, and it takes getting used to. I was suffering with the change. Nine days into the camp…

From My Journal

> *My fencing is just <u>ugly</u> right now! My legs aren't working right. I'm tired. I can't breathe this thin air. This is not fun; it's like being sentenced to hard labor.*

> *My emotions are <u>negative.</u> My mood is <u>zero.</u>*

I started to get a little paranoid. I began to think that

Perekalski was plotting to mess me up so he could select Grigoriev instead of me. One day, he asked me if I'd like to fence in some junior national tournament. I thought, *he just wants me out of here. He wants me off the team.* I told him no thanks.

On July 23, we had a training competition: nine of us started out in three pools of three. I lost both of my pool bouts and was relegated to the "C" pool, the losers' pool. There I won one bout, but lost to Grigoriev, 5 – 0. I had tears in my eyes.

From My Journal

Apathy. I don't want to fence! My mouth is dry. I can't sense the distance....

I hadn't guessed it, but I should have. Once again, I was overtrained. The mountains were getting to me. Just because I was still on the team by points (actually, I was much lower than fifth in the standings), that didn't mean I was going to Denver. The trainers could say I was simply in rotten shape, that I couldn't take the altitude. They could still leave me back in the USSR, watching television.

But we're still in the middle of that training competition, where, with one victory in the "C" pool, I was seeded a "glorious" eighth of the nine fencers. At least I was still in it! I had to fence Shevchenko, the number one seed.

There was no way I could fence this one as if it were just another practice session. For me, this was the most important tournament of my life. I beat Shevchenko 10 – 7, *just because I had to.* In the semis I had Kliushin, who (remember?) had roared back from a 9 – 5 deficit to beat me in the USSR championship. It was exactly the same scenario this time—but the result was the reverse. This time he had me down 9 – 5, and I beat him 11 – 9. After that, the championship bout was a piece of cake. I beat Koretski 10 – 4...

... and was walking on air.

Now I needed an American visa. Actually, all of us did, but with the combination of Soviet and American bureaucracy, nothing was certain. Every day, during our lesson, I'd ask Perekalski whether I was going to get the visa or not, and every day, he'd say, "Probably." It made me nervous. I pictured my visa being "accidentally misplaced" so that someone else would have to take my place. I was almost sure of it.

After the camp, we flew to Moscow. I went to Valerian Bazarevich, our FIE member, and asked him whether I'd be going. "Probably," he said.

I'd had it.

I went to Perekalski and ranted to him that I was going home, I was taking a night train to Kiev, I wouldn't stay another day.

"Hold on," he said, and picked up a telephone.

A few minutes later, he told me that our passports were in order. We'd all be getting them at the airport. The Soviet team chief, Galina Gorokhova, who had three Olympic team gold medals to her credit, would deliver the precious documents. A wave of relief swept over me.

But at the airport, Gorokhova didn't arrive, and the gates were starting to close. It was a US airline—Pan Am— and they weren't going to delay their flight for a miserable bunch of Soviet fencers. But with minutes to spare…

… Gorokhova miraculously appeared!

I was on my way to the World Championships at last.

Denver 1989

We flew in a Boeing 747, an airplane I had only seen in movies. I could hardly believe that a thing that big could fly. During the flight, I asked the stewardess for a beer. Romankov, who was sitting next to me, didn't say anything. He just gave me a long, dirty look. After that, the beer didn't taste good any more.

> I asked the steward-ess for a beer.
> Romankov shot me a long, dirty look.

We were met at New York's JFK airport by a limousine. All of us went crazy—it had a telephone, a TV...and even a bar! Even in a movie, none of us had seen anything like it.

And when we got to Denver, where I shared a suite with Boris Koretski, we literally couldn't believe what we found: there were *three TV's—including one in the bathroom.* Capitalism!

In Denver, I met up with my buddy Thomas Endres. I saw that he was surprised to see me on the team. So were the other fencers and team captains. Nobody had ever seen me at a senior World Cup. Most of them had never even heard my name. Who was this Golubitsky and what was he doing on the mighty Soviet team?

As for me, I was proud of myself and tried to stay cool, but it wasn't easy. I didn't feel that my own team accepted me, let alone the rest of the world. I was number five, though. In principle, I could be a simple tourist, just along for the ride, warming the bench during serious matches. Face it: they didn't need me, but I needed them very much.

Shortly after our arrival, the foil team held a business meeting to fix the price of all the stuff we had brought to sell—caviar, blades, equipment. For example, the price of a Maraging steel blade was set at forty US dollars. **Problem!**

There was this guy from Chile whom I'd known for two years. Day after day, he begged me to drop the price, complaining about his financial woes. He swore he'd never tell a soul. Finally, I let him have two blades for $70.00. Blades in hand, he walked out of the room—and bumped into Mamedov, who asked him a couple of searching questions. A few minutes later, Mamedov stormed into my room and punched me in the stomach, not gently.

Romankov was there too. All he said was, "In the future, kid, your services may no longer be required." I was shaking inside.

Meanwhile, I was fencing well in practice, but I was still troubled by the nosebleeds and fatigue brought on by the altitude. I didn't practice for two days before the individuals, hoping that the rest would refresh me.

Finally, the day I had been dreaming about arrived.

In the first round, I lost just one bout, to Howe of East Germany, and had a good win over Benny Wendt of Austria. Now, Benny is a friend of mine. In normal life, he's a great guy. Every time we meet, we have fun—off the strip. But he is a really unpleasant person to fence against because he tries to win at any cost. Any win over him is a good win.

In the second round, I lost only to Mauro Numa, the very great Italian (after his fencing career ended, we became good buddies).

In the third round of pools, I ran into a bunch of "Highlanders"—warrior immortals—including Matthias Gey of West Germany, the 1987 World Champion; Stefano Cerioni of Italy, the 1988 Olympic Champion; the '88 Silver Medalist Udo Wagner; the top Hungarian, who had beaten me every time we fenced, and...oh yes, Elvis Gregory of Cuba. My teammates gave me their condolences. Thanks for the vote of confidence, guys!

> In the third round, I ran into a bunch of "Highlanders,"

Gey, approached me at the start of the pool, asked me, "Last bout?" I said yes, like an idiot, but I had no idea what he meant. Afterwards, Boris Koretski explained it to me. If we had a "last bout?" agreement, whoever needed the bout could ask for it before fencing the last bout, and the other would just let him through, with no further obligations in future rounds.

"What if we both need it?" I asked.

"You just fight for it, then," said Boris.

Fortunately, Matthias didn't ask me for anything. I probably would have said no, which would have been a great start for my senior international career!

We fenced the pool. I beat Gregory 5 – 2, Gey 5 – 1, Szekeres 5 – 4, and went up. In another pool, Ilgar Mamedov was the victim of a "last bout" deal. He had a deal with Andrea Borella and asked for the bout, but Borella wouldn't let him win. Mamedov was furious, but of course there was nothing he could do. For him, the individual championship was over.

Flushed with my success in the pools, I hit the wall in the direct elimination table, losing to Piotr Kielpikowski of Poland 7 – 10 and Andrea Cipressa of Italy 6 – 10, taking 25th place. I finished twenty-fifth, and honestly, I was not at all satisfied. I knew I could have done better.

Dmitri Shevchenko was the only Soviet to make it to the final of eight, losing in the quarters to Alex Koch, who eventually beat Philippe Omnès of France for the World Championship.

It hadn't been a great day for Soviet fencing.

You'll remember that Perekalski was calling me "kid" all the time. It really got on my nerves. Before the team event I went up to him.

"If I become a world champion, will you stop calling me *kid*?"

If I become a World Champion, will you stop calling me *Kid*?

"If you become a world champion, *Kid*, I'll call you *Grandpa!*"

"Grandpa is a bit much. Just

110

drop the "Kid" and I'll be happy."

"When you're a world champion, I'll stop calling you Kid."

Now there was an incentive!

July 8 was the first day of the team event. We beat Japan 9 – 3 and Israel 9 – 1. I fenced five bouts and won them all.

Next came the quarterfinals. We were up against a very strong East German team, and as the number five man, I was riding the bench. Koretski didn't like to fence the Germans—something about their style. He ran into problems and lost two bouts.

Perekalski looked over at me. "Kid, start warming up." I went out and beat Wagner and Roemer, both by 5 – 1 margins.

In the semis, we faced Italy, one of the favorites for the gold. I went up to Perekalski.

"Listen, Coach, I'm not scared, but I just want you to know that I lost three bouts to Italians in the individuals."

So our wise coach benched me again.

Fortunately, this time—unlike with the East Germans—Koretski was invincible. He won all four of his bouts in a 9 – 6 victory. Now we could prepare ourselves for the final against West Germany. There was a break of a few hours, and we went back to our hotel.

While I was resting in my room, Koretski came in, looking solemn. "Kid, you have to come with me," he said.

A little nervously, I followed him.

In the next room was the whole foil squad, standing around a table with a row of glasses on it, filled to the brim.

Romankov spoke first. "Kid, we have a long tradition on this team. Before the final, we all chug one vodka for

"We have a tradition—we all chug a glass of vodka for luck."

I looked at the full tumbler in front of me.

> "What do I do against him, Boris?"
> "Just be yourself. Fence the way you always do."

good luck."

I think my eyes got big. I could feel the gaze of the veterans upon me.

"No problem!" I said cheerfully, and poured the liquid down my throat.

I almost choked...at the explosion of laughter around the room.

The glass was full of water!

It was a stupid, harmless joke, but it broke the tension completely. I felt just as good as if I had passed a real initiation. I felt accepted, part of the team at last. And I thought it was because I didn't fence like a wuss, but like a man.

We got to the tournament venue early, to warm up and check our weapons. I could feel the pressure build. I was in reserve, but Koretski still didn't like to fence Germans, losing to Endres and Koch.

"Kid, it's your turn," said Perekalski.

I was up against Thorsten Weidner.

"What do I do against him?" I asked Boris.

He gave me some advice, but then he looked at me. "Just fence the way you always fence," he told me. "Be yourself!"

The match score was 4 – 4 when I went onto the strip. I was as nervous as I had ever been in my life. I made seven off-target hits in a row before I got a colored light to go on. In the end, I brought home the precious win, 5 – 3.

Next time I was up, we had the lead, 7 – 6, but I had to fence Matthias Gey. My first touch was simple and brilliant: I made two false simple attacks, slightly short to avoid his riposte. I was hypnotizing him into taking a parry. Then I started straight in again...

And he went for it!

Waiting for exactly the right moment, I hit him with a coupé while his parry bit the air. It was like an exercise in a lesson. I was in the zone, winning the bout 5 – 3 and pushing the score to 8 – 6.

One bout later, with the score 8 – 7, Shevchenko faced Koch in the bout that would decide the championship. Would Dima be able to revenge his defeat in the quarters of the individuals?

Yes!

Alex had no chance that day as Dima took care of business, 5 – 1. He had won all four of his bouts. Romankov had won three. I had won two.

We were the world champions!

I was a world champion!!

I felt as if I could lift the Earth. I was laughing and crying at the same time.

That night, back at the hotel, we celebrated our victory. This time, the vodka was real.

But before that, another tradition had to be observed. Romankov and Koretski spanked me with the biggest slippers they could find (Shevchenko's).

The first time you fence for the Soviet team, you have to be baptized!

I felt great. I was one of "them" now.

Later, I asked Perekalski to stop calling me Kid. And he did.

We landed at Moscow airport, slightly intoxicated with an unforgettable mixture of joy and alcohol. Incredibly, beautifully, we were met by a sea of flowers, smiles, reporters. It was like a fantasy. I reminded myself that I was just one member of a team. I had helped a bit—that was all.

Then I heard Romankov—the great Romankov—giving an interview. "We wouldn't have won without Golubitsky," he said. I cherished these words from one of the greatest fencers in the history of our sport.

I even forgave him for spoiling the taste of my beer on the plane to New York.

I had started the season by going into the Red Army. I was a junior fencer. I had done 161 days of camps, training from one to three times a day, traveling all the time, with scarcely a free day to just relax. I had worked, but I had some luck, too. Two Olympic champions were off the team that season.

Still, I had managed to make the team, proving that *luck is what we make of it.*

I had never looked back. I saw my star in the sky and I was moving toward it without reservations. I didn't have anything to lose, so all I could do was win.

> You must believe that you are the only factor in striving for your ultimate goal. Hard work and belief can work miracles!
>
> **You can—you will— do it!**

I realize that most of you who read this book don't have my opportunity to train and travel. But you still must understand—believe—that you and you alone are the only factor in striving for your own ultimate goal.

Hard work and belief can work miracles.

You can—you will—do it!

I had no idea then, but it would take me another two years to achieve my individual goal.

Warming Up at the Junior World Chmpionships
Athens, 1989

In the Army (1988)

*My First World Cup Final of Eight
Venice, 1990*

On the Cusp

1989—1990

I came back home to my lovely Kiev and had a few precious days to celebrate my success. After being in the army for a year, I had the right to continue my studies at the University. I transferred to correspondence courses, so that I could keep up with my studies while training and competing. I won two minor tournaments, one in Ukraine and another in Portugal. At the end of October, I would compete in the first serious all-Soviet tournament of the 1989-90 season: the USSR Cup. After a two week camp with the Ukrainian team, I went to Tashkent, Uzbekistan, where the Cup was to be held.

This would be a very significant competition for me. True, I was a team World Champion, but that was *last* season. In addition, Aptsiauri and Ibragimov were back in contention. They wanted to take back "their" places on the team. Between seven and nine people would be trying to grab seats in a car that held only four. (I say 'only four,' even though there would be five on the team, because Romankov was going to be on the team automatically — that was how good he was then.) I felt that the struggle would be much harder than it had been last season. Then, I had sort of sneaked onto the team. Now, from the very start of this new season, my results would have to be very convincing if I wanted to make that top four. I was sure that my rivals would watch me, study me, and try to outdo me. It made me really nervous. I felt that I needed at least to reach the final eight in this competition if I wanted to get the year off to a good start. I felt that I was under serious pressure.

I fenced pretty well in the pools, but lost to Ibragimov in the direct elimination table. I would have to beat Ilgar Mamedov in the repechage to make the final eight. And here I got really lucky. The score was 9 – 9. Just one touch… I made an attack; Ilgar took a parry four and riposted. All I could do was remise, out of time. I didn't scream, because I knew that I had lost. He didn't scream, because he knew he had won.

The referee made only one mistake throughout the bout. Right then. For me. He said that I had made a beat attack. Mamedov was shocked. Me too. I had made it to the final at his expense.

I guess I was satisfied with my result, because I lost to Shaimardanov and took fifth place. Let me tell you who was in that final: Grigoriev, Shaimardanov, Aptsiauri, Shevchenko, Ibragimov, Koretski, Sladkov and I. Mamedov ended ninth — almost all the candidates for the USSR team were there. (Romankov didn't fence in that competition)

A few weeks later, the Ukrainian team went to Katowice, Poland. I took second place, losing in the final to the Polish fencer Bandach (referee problems!). I was fencing fairly well when one of Polish coaches approached me.

"You are doing a good job," he said.

I responded: "Of course, what do you think? *I'm a World Champion!*"

What arrogance!

Even now, years later, the Polish fencers and I are still laughing about that dumb remark.

The next competition was the first senior World Cup of my life. At that time, the FIE (International Fencing

Federation) was experimenting with different competition formats. In this one, there would be a final of six people.

In my last bout before the final, I had to face Uli Schreck of West Germany for the best of three five-touch bouts. The first was his, 5 – 2; the second was mine, 5 – 3. In the third, we were at three touches apiece. I had never fenced against Uli before and had no idea of his style and mentality. He drove me crazy, by... *staying cool and calm.* He showed absolutely no emotions, no screaming. I just didn't get it. I was waiting for the moment when he would get nervous or angry or excited. His calm made *me* nervous. I lost 5 – 3. I wound up in eighth place and didn't make the podium.

> He drove me crazy... by staying calm. It made me nervous.

The next day we fenced the team competition. I was very proud to be fencing for the USSR first team, together with Shevchenko, Koretski, Mamedov and Grigoriev.

I spent four years with the USSR team. These were the last four years of the team, because the USSR ceased to exist in 1991 and the team disbanded after the 1992 Olympics. I was always proud to compete for the USSR team, and the team always made me proud of it.

This was true in individual competitions, but especially true in the team events, where we were competing for each other and for the USSR, rather than for ourselves. I felt a mixture of heavy responsibility and great honor. This heady blend pushed me to make myself almost invincible. In fact, I rarely lost when fencing in team events. I felt that if I stumbled, my teammates would "have my back"—my next teammate would immediately make up for my loss. But at the same time, I felt that I had *no right to lose.* I didn't want to see a teammate having to make up for my weakness.

In the quarters of that World Cup, we fenced against Italy. I hadn't had good results against the Italians in last year's World Championships. But it was my day. I beat them all after each other! That meant a lot to me, giving me confidence that I could fence with the Italians and beat them when it counted. In the semis we beat the USSR second team. In the final we fenced France. And again, as with the Italians, I won all four bouts. I was fencing for the first time in my life against most of them. They had to remember my name after that. At least, I hoped so.

At the end of the day, I had won all sixteen of the bouts I fenced.

Now that I had been on that World Championships team, I started to get some perks that made my life more comfortable. For example, I no longer had to do my military service in western Ukraine every three months In fact, the last time I went there was right after the Worlds. My commanders treated me well. A few times, they even lined up the troops and had me talk to them. I didn't really know what I had to say, because just a few months earlier, I had been one of them. So I just told them, actually, more or less what I wrote at the end of previous chapter, that everything was up to them. It was in their hands.

"If you want to succeed in sport, you have to go all the way. You have to believe in your success," I told them.

I was going to have to work hard to make the USSR team. But things kept getting in the way. One time the team was having a camp in Byelorussia before the USSR Tournament of the Strongest. Just before it was to start, I had to take my driver's test. I had informed Alexandr Perekalski, that I would arrive one day late to the camp, knowing that he hated to see anyone be late, whether or not he had a valid reason. He kept iron discipline on the national team.

I took the test and failed it (I passed it later). After the test, I went to the airport to fly to Minsk. I got to the Kiev well before departure and picked up a book to pass the time. I kept looking at my ticket as the flights were called. My flight number was, let's say 472B. After a while, I heard the call for Flight 472. I looked up at the screen, and saw that the letter "B" was missing, so I went back to my book.

After a while, I checked my watch. It was getting very close to the scheduled departure time, to fly, but Flight 472B never appeared. I went to the information window with my ticket to ask what was going on. The pretty flight attendant told me that my flight was full. I was too late. I had been messed up by that one missing letter! I wanted to laugh at myself for being so stupid, and at the same time I knew that Perekalski was really going to kick my butt.

By a small miracle, I got my money back for the airline ticket, grabbed a taxi to the railroad station, bought a train ticket to Minsk and arrived at the camp...two days late.

The tournament was held in the sports complex in Staiki, near Minsk, in a country setting of great natural beauty. Once again, the tournament used its traditional two-day format.

I was ill before the tournament (perhaps because of the stress of travel), being feverish and sleepless the night before the event. But as weak as I felt, I managed to take first on both days of the tournament, leaving all the "big guys" behind me. It was my first outright victory in one of the most difficult competitions in the USSR. In this case, the pressure seems to have been good for me. The fear of not making the team was a good motivation factor, making me stronger, making me push myself to the limit.

Next up was the Venice World Cup. I had known Venice's reputation as a beautiful city, but the reality took my breath away. The wonderful ancient palazzos by the canals were unforgettable.

I don't remember whether I was nervous or not, probably I was. But, as always, the first few touches in the first pool, I was focused and ready.

To get into the final eight I had to fence Matthias Behr of W. Germany. Almost eight years ago, my hero, Vladimir

Smirnov, had fenced against Matthias in the tragic last bout that took his life. For me, this was early in my international fencing career. For Matthias, it would be his last season. Maybe it sounds stupid, but I wanted to win this bout not only for myself, but for Smirnov's memory. And I won, two bouts to one, making my first World Cup final.

Two other Soviets made it to that top eight: Shevchenko and Mamedov. In the semis I had to fence Dmitri Shevchenko. That year, he had a very good chance that season of winning the overall World Cup—being tops in the rankings for the whole year. I decided to give him the bout. I did this without telling Dmitri or my own coach. Instead, I went to Dmitri's coach, Mark Midler, and told him that I would let "Dima" win.

The first action was simultaneous attacks. I touched his arm; he missed me by a mile. As we passed, I had time to whisper, "Just touch me!" On the next simultaneous action I missed and he tore my electric vest apart. Nice! Of course I lost that match. For third place I got to fence Ilgar Mamedov. I won the first bout and was leading 4 – 2 in second. There was just one touch between me and the podium. But Ilgar turned on his turbos and gave me no chance whatsoever. I was kept off the podium, taking fourth place after losing two bouts to one.

That world cup in Venice would be one of the very few good individual results I over the next few seasons, although our Dinamo team won the team European Cup in Paris, and I felt great about that. I fenced very well when I fought for a team, but I wasn't ready to fence for myself yet.

During the 1989-90 season, I fenced tournaments in Paris, Bonn and Budapest but finished very far from the top. The coaches and fencers of all of the rival different teams had begun to study me and my fencing style, discovering my weak spots and using them against me. I had to be patient, training hard, trying to stick with my style and wait for my day to arrive. I had to get more experience. My consolation was that most of my rivals for the USSR Olympic team weren't doing much better. Only Shevchenko and Romankov were doing well. As a result, I knew that fencing well within the USSR could be my ticket to the World Championships.

At this stage of my career, I was still green—just another promising, hardworking junior. I still didn't know when to take a time out during a bout. In addition, I felt that I had to fence every competition at 110%. I was afraid that if I wasn't really much stronger

> I was still very green at this time. I didn't know when to take a time out; I felt that I had to fence at 110% all the time. I couldn't plan my season.

than my teammates, I would be left home. That meant that I couldn't really plan my season—decide which tournaments would be "just for the experience" and which ones I would go all out. So I went all out throughout the whole season and had to pay the price in injuries.

The last important qualification competition of the season, the USSR Championships, would take place this year in Kiev. I had been a twelve-year old beginner when I watched Smirnov take the title in Kiev, in the very same venue where we were going to fence this year. I wanted to win in Kiev too: it would be very special to win it in my hometown.

Grigoriev, Mamedov, Shevchenko, Romankov, Koretski, a couple of juniors, and I were in the final eight. I had to fence against the great Romankov in the quarters, so I warmed up for ages. I took a lesson with my dad an hour and half before the final. The lesson went on forever, with only a couple of breaks. Before our bout, I was dead. I was exhausted after the long warm up and lost my sharpness. Romankov beat me 5 – 3, 5 – 3. I made too many flat ripostes. I was really disappointed that I couldn't match Smirnov's win, but I was happy enough that I had confirmed my standing by finishing in the top four.

In the final, Grigoriev beat Mamedov, with Romankov taking third place.

The last camp before World Championship in Lyon, France was back in Staiki, Belarus. In the beginning I had the same traditional complaints: bleeding nose, tiredness, injured ankle. As much as possible, I tried to sleep and take outdoor walks in order to stay fresh. By the end of camp, I felt more or less OK, but not really perfect. My left elbow had begun to hurt. Every time I scored a touch, I felt a sharp pain. I had "tennis elbow," that is, tendonitis of the elbow. For many years to come, I would fence with this pain, trying to deal with it. Especially it would hurt the most at the end of each season, right before the World Championships. On top of that, I developed a pain in my shoulder. Sometimes it hurt so much I couldn't lift my left arm. I now realize that I was paying the price for using the flick, which stresses the joints, muscles, and ligaments much more than the classical techniques.

When you're young, you refuse to give in to injury. You are in a hurry. You think that injuries are just temporary. You pay for that thinking later on. To avoid injury, you need to take enough time to warm up and stretch. To minimize the damage when you are injured, you need to take enough time to rest and recuperate, to take massages and heat treatments, to do what is necessary to recover.

> I suffered for years from tendinitis of the elbow—the price of using the flick.
> When you're young, you think that injuries are just temporary. Later, you pay for that thinking.

The doctors on our team would try to do everything possible to help me out, but I always rejected cortisone injections. I thought that they would be only half measures:

Maybe I would get rid of the pain for a while, but I would pay a double price later on. The cortisone shot would take the pain away without solving the problem. I could fence in a tournament, using my injured shoulder and elbow at 100%, but afterwards, the pain would be back, twice as strong. I preferred to fence with pain. That way, I knew exactly when I was damaging myself and I could try to deal with it.

The USSR team was announced a week before our departure; it consisted (in rank order) of Shevchenko, me, Romankov, Aptsiauri, Koretski. I had finished second after Shevchenko, but ahead of three Olympic Champions! I had to count my first season among the seniors as successful.

Our trip to Lyon wasn't easy. After flying from Moscow to Paris, we spent hours waiting for our train in the Gare de Lyon. We arrived at our hotel late and out of sorts.

This time I felt that more people were watching me. Fencers would stop for a while to watch my lesson with Perekalski. However, going into the individuals, I still didn't feel much pressure on my shoulders because I was concentrating on staying in shape for the team event.

After the pools, I had a very tough DE table. I won my first match, against Ye Chong of China, with difficulty, 5 – 6, 5 – 3, 5 – 1. After the bout, I wrote

From my journal:

I was dead from the start—from the first bout to the last.

I guess it was a result of overtraining. I didn't have enough experience to rest at the right moment so that I would get to the tournament at my 100% best.

In my next bout, I lost to my friend Thomas Endres 0 – 2 (4 – 6, 1 – 5). To make top 8 from the repechage (second chance table for losers), I had to win my next four matches. I beat the Hungarian Nemeth (5 – 2, 3 – 5, 5 – 0), my team-mate Aptsiauri (5 – 3, 6 – 4) and the great Mauro Numa of Italy (5 – 3, 6 – 5). To make the final of eight, I had to beat Italy's tall Andrea Borella, the 1986 World Champion and winner of many World Cup events. However, I could do nothing against him, losing 0 – 5, 3 – 5 and taking ninth place.

It was progress compared to last year's result: I had jumped from twenty-fifth place to ninth.

Borella finished second after Omnès of France; Shevchenko took third place and won the overall World Cup. Amazingly, I finished number nine in the world ranking, missing the top 8 by just one point. The first eight would fence later in a Masters' Tournament, where you could earn some money. Who knows, if I hadn't given the bout to Shevchenko in Venice, I might have been able to get there. But this is just a "what if" —no one cares anymore.

In the team event, we beat the USA, Turkey, and Romania in the qualification round. Then, in the quarter-finals, we beat Korea 9 – 1. In the semis we met Italy. Just like the year before, I was in reserve. We lost the first four bouts before Perekalski let me fence. I beat Puccini 5 – 4 in my only bout (he finished in top 8 in the individuals), but the Italian team took revenge for last year's defeat, winning 8 – 7 with a huge touch difference.

For third place, we beat West Germany 9 – 4. In my three bouts I received only one touch, from Thorsten Weidner, whitewashing Matthias Gey and Uli Schreck. That pleased me, of course, and it was nice to get the third place team medal, I guess; but none of us felt genuinely happy.

1990—1991

Preparation for the new 1990-91 season started from the camp in Sukhumi, Republic of Georgia. We went there without our fencing bags. This camp would consist only of athletic preparation and footwork.

At night, most of the fencers would get together and party. We were drinking fine Georgian wine, which is made from some of the oldest grape varieties in the word, and is winning an international reputation. (Jason probably drank Georgian wine when he went there to search for the Golden Fleece and wound up with a Georgian princess named Medea.) We were also drinking chacha, which tastes like the French marc or the Italian grappa. Good chacha is supposed to be smoother than grappa; bad chacha is another story. Both kinds are about ninety proof. We were drinking the home-made kind, which wasn't too bad. (What do you need when you're young?) Then, in the middle of the night, we would take a swim in the Black sea. Afternoons we mostly played football (again, that's soccer to you Americans). Our masseur always used to prepare us a 10 liter tank of sport drink. Every few minutes most of us would take a few sips from it, being thirsty after the party.

Every night, the same tank would be filled with wine.

Listen, I know that this is completely unacceptable as a training method! But I was young. I felt at the time that I had to drink with the veteran team members or be looked at as a geek (or as we said in Russian, a "white crow.")

The USSR Cup, this time held in Nikolaev, Ukraine, opened the fencing season. We had to fence in an aluminum field house with a rubber surface for track and field. All the main contenders made the final. The bout that would determine the last of the eight finalists was underway. The bout seemed to go on forever, with the fencers taking numerous breaks. The weather was really warm, and the rubber track was sending its fumes into the air. Everybody got a little dizzy.

But on top of that, some of the fencers had been doing some serious partying the night before the event, and now they were paying the price. The bout had been going on for nearly twenty minutes, when one of the fencers stamped his foot for a time out and asked the referee, "Excuse me, can I puke?"

The ref looked at him with eyes full of deep understanding, and said "Oh, yes! Of course!"

The poor guy took only a few steps off the strip and threw up. Then he won the bout and made the final eight!

The next event (after a two-week training camp, of course) was the World Cup in Leningrad. I took 11th place, losing to the great Mauro Numa 1 – 5, 5 – 3, 5 – 6.

On December 29, 1990, I finally fulfilled a vow that was now more than a year old. Before the 1989 World Championships, I had made a promise that if I became a world champion, I would get baptized. I didn't know the Bible saying, "Thou shalt not put the Lord thy God to the test," meaning you shouldn't say if I get this or that, *then* I'll believe in God. So I made the promise.

My dream came true and I kept my word. I was baptized in a tiny Catholic church at the far end of Kiev. I didn't know the priest or anyone else who was present.

Ukraine is a mostly Orthodox country, but for some reason that I don't understand, I wanted to be a Catholic. I don't know why. I have nothing against the Orthodox faith or any other. Your faith, your true church, is not in the building, but in your heart.

The next World Cup was in Havana, Cuba. It was my first visit to this country—a country of contrasts. I liked this island very much. Every time I visit, it somehow gives me energy and strength. I love the relaxed lifestyle and the friendly people.

To make the final eight, I had to fence Luca Vitalesta of Italy. I still remember the match as if it were yesterday. The score stood at one bout apiece. I was concentrating for the last decisive bout. I told myself that I had to give 110% of my physical and mental abilities if I wanted to win this one. I believed that you can't make the final easily. You have to give more than you can. This time it worked. I won 5 – 3 and made the second World Cup final in my career. I finished fourth, Ibragimov fifth, Koretski seventh. I was holding my own among the contenders for the USSR team.

After Havana (and another camp) came the USSR Tournament of the Strongest. It still had its unique format: we fenced two competitions on consecutive days and the trophy would go to the fencer with the highest two-day total. On the first day, I had Ilgar Mamedov and Boris Koretski in my third-round pool. We made a deal for a "happy round," so that no one would have to work too hard and no one would fall too far behind. I gave a bout to Koretski, Mamedov gave a bout to me, and Koretski gave a bout to Mamedov.

But Boris Koretski made a mistake: he made a *second* deal, with one of the juniors in the pool. Boris and the junior would fence to 4 – 4, and then Boris, of course, would win. They fenced to 4 – 4. As agreed, they fenced to 4 – 4. Koretski signaled to the kid that they would do simultaneous attacks and the kid should miss.

Koretski didn't see that Igor Vainberg was standing behind his back. Vainberg was doing a little pantomime: "Win it, kid! Go for it!" So as Koretski went in with his straight lunge, the kid made a parry-riposte and beat him. All of us broke up laughing, except Boris.

I met Shevchenko in the final. I went to Mark Midler, his coach, and asked for the bout back, reminding him of my gift to Shevchenko in Venice. On the second day I had to fence Koretski in the final. We flipped a coin for the bout. I called heads, and heads it was. As the first-place finisher on both days, I had won the tournament. It was a great start to the season: eighth at the USSR Cup, fourth at the World Cup in Cuba, first in the Tournament of the Strongest. It was only February, but I had a great chance at making the team for the World Championships in Budapest.

But the rest of the international season wasn't very good for me. I fenced in four World Cup tournaments; twice making only the top sixty-four twice and twice only the top thirty-two. It was awful.

I guess that it just wasn't my time yet. The level of world foil was very high, and I was just one of many fencers who were capable of occasional good results.

The only bright spot came, as usual, at a team event, the Seven Nations tournament. The top seven teams from the last World Championships, plus a second German team, would meet in Germany for this prestigious event. The Soviet team consisted of Shevchenko, Ibragimov, Mamedov, Koretski and me.

At the outset, I couldn't find my game. I was fighting myself, and not my opponents, getting angrier and angrier at myself. At one point I stormed out of the competition area and broke down in tears. I didn't believe that I could fence at all any more. Ilgar Mamedov went out after me to calm me down.

"It's OK," he said. "You'll get the feeling back." But the frustration of fencing poorly at all those World Cups had gotten the better of me.

"I'll never fence well again," I said despairingly. I needed to lash out. I saw a board lying on the ground and I kicked it.

The pain was incredible. I thought I had broken my foot. I limped back into the fencing venue, and...suddenly I was fencing really well! All my doubts had somehow dropped far behind me. I won almost all my bouts. Mamedov was right: the feeling had come back.

Meanwhile, the big world outside was breaking in on the little world of fencing. The Berlin Wall that separated East and West Germany had dramatically fallen on November 9, 1989. There were no longer two Germanys. This season there was a single, unified German team. They beat us but lost to Italy, whom we beat, creating a three-way tie which we won by having the best won-lost differential. Individually, I took third after Numa and Weidner. Things were starting to look up again!

Two weeks later we had the Spartakiad of the Soviet Union in Leningrad. The winner would take the USSR Championship. All the best were there. My dad was the chief of Ukrainian team. I made the final 8 and had to fence in the quarters against Bryzgalov, another Ukrainian, my father's student, in quarters. I won 5 – 3, 5 – 3 for the right to cross foils with Dmitri Kazakov of Uzbekistan.

With the score tied at one bout each, we were both exhausted. He looked tired; I felt as if I were dying. The score was 2 – 2, when I heard the voice of my opponent's teammate calling to him: "Dmitri,

> My opponent's teammate called out that I was tired. That gave me new energy!

he's tired!" I turned my head to find who said those words. They gave me a burst of energy that drove me to score three consecutive touches in a matter of seconds, ending the bout 5 – 2 and propelling me to the final. There I had to fence Mamedov, who could do nothing against me. I seized the gold of the Spartakiad and the title of champion of the USSR.

In the team event, Ukraine took the bronze. I was happy for my dad and my teammates: The Ukrainian foil team hadn't known such success for many years.

This year would be the year of the. World University Games (also called the Universiade) in Sheffield, England, which is a great worldwide sports festival like a mini-

Olympics. To be able to participate I had to fence in the all-Soviet Student Games in Kharkov, Ukraine. I reserved my ticket to the University games by beating Grigoriev in the semis and Oganesian in the final.

Meanwhile, we had to train for the World Championships in Budapest. Romankov hadn't had a great season. He was already almost thirty-eight years of age, but still ranked fifth in the world point standings. Romankov, Shevchenko, Mamedov, Ibragimov and I would represent our country at the World Championships. At those championships, Shevchenko and Ibragimov made the final eight, while I failed to show anything extraordinary, losing to a Korean and to Elvis Gregory to take thirty-first.

In team another disappointment awaited: we would lose to Germany in the semis and to France for the bronze.

A month later I scooped up a whole bunch of medals at the University Games. I finished in the top eight in individual foil and our team placed second, after Italy, in the foil team event. On top of this, I won team silver and bronze as a reserve in epee and sabre!

I finished season ranked first in Soviet men's' foil. I'd had a few results in international tournaments. But I still knew that something was lacking. I felt that I wasn't that far from being among the best in the world, but that I still needed … it—that certain something. "It" in my case, would prove to be patience and belief in myself.

The End of the USSR

The fall of the Berlin Wall had unleashed a series of momentous events. One by one, the countries of Eastern Europe rejected Communism. The Soviet economy was in crisis. The Soviet Union pulled its troops out of Afghanistan after almost two decades of futile occupation. Mikhail Gorbachev, who had won the Nobel Peace Prize, was now preparing to promulgate a new constitution shifting more power to the republics. A small group of hard-liners within the government believed that Gorbachev's rule would destroy the country and the communist idea. In August 1991 while Gorbachev was vacationing in the Crimea, they made their move. They cut off his telephone communications, demanded his resignation, declared a state of emergency, and sent tanks toward Moscow and Kiev. It was a bid to use fear in order to turn the clock back.

But people didn't want to kneel down before this coup. Protestors took to the streets, defying the tanks. These were the days when Boris Yeltsin, the President of the Russian Republic, made himself into a symbol of freedom. You could see him on the barricades talking to people, giving an example of courage. In a few days, the farce had ended. In the Crimea, Gorbachev had refused to sign the resignation papers and returned to Moscow an apparent winner. But in fact, he had lost control over the Soviet Union. Yeltsin, as head of the largest state of the USSR, now held the strongest hand.

Gorbachev was now a king without a kingdom. In a televised speech, he resigned and recommended the end of the Communist Party. In a surprisingly short time, Yeltsin had presided over the end of the USSR. Within just seven days, seventy-four years of Communist rule had come to an end.

Within a few months, the former republics declared their independence. Kravchuk became the leader of Ukraine; Shushkevich took the leadership in Belarus. These leaders decided to form the "Commonwealth of Independent States."

These immense events changed the political order of the world and the destiny of hundreds of millions of people. They also impacted the little world of what had been Soviet sport.

I had begun the season, with my teammates and rivals, as a member of the mighty USSR team. I had—we all had—been born in a country that no longer existed! We had been

> We had spent our careers for a country that no longer existed. We were a team without a country.

spending our athletic careers for a country that no longer existed. Who could have imagined that? We would compete in the Olympics as members of the "Unified Team," a team without a country, a team that had not existed before and would never exist again.

Within the world of sports—as elsewhere—it was deeply, personally, shocking.

Back in the new nation of Ukraine, the nationalists wanted the Ukrainian contingent at the Barcelona Olympics to compete as a separate national team. There were strong debates about this during the months before the Olympics, but most of us athletes, who had been members of the Soviet team throughout our athletic careers, were deeply against the separation. Thank God, it never happened.

1991—1992

As I said, I'd ended the previous season feeling that I was close to where I wanted to be, but that something was lacking.

I'd like to talk a bit more about the meaning of this mysterious "it". "It" has many synonyms: hard work, belief in oneself, patience, heroism, talent, sacrifice. We hear many times (not just in sports) that someone could have had better results but never did. He lacked "it." Having "it" or not divides athletes into two groups: the elite, the legends, and "he's not so bad..."

In the 1992 Olympic season, I finally got "it" for a moment, after many years of training, in the USSR Cup, the first event of the season. I remember nothing about it except that it was held in Kishinev, the capital of Moldova, and that I won.

After the USSR Cup and one more two-week camp, the

Soviet team headed to Vienna for a World Cup. Newspaper articles after this one would talk about my "killer instinct."

It was November 24, 1991. I made the final eight for only the third time in my life. There were six Germans, the Austrian Anatol Richter, and me. In the quarters, I beat Thomas Endres 6 – 5, 5 – 2; in the semis I beat Uli Schreck 1 – 5, 6 – 4, 5 – 1. In the final Ingo Weissenborn, the 1991 World Champion, would examine me.

I won first bout 5 – 1 and led 4 – 1 in the second. Trying to stay focused, I screamed out: "Touch! One touch!" I thought about the times when I couldn't make just that one touch, the last touch. Now I refocused on the task a hand. I didn't let myself think about first place, even for a second. I made an attack and immediately remised with opposition. One light! I win!

I got congratulations from many athletes and coaches. I gave my first interview to foreign journalists. I was so happy. After the doping control, I went to the hotel, where we celebrated my success.

The next World Cup was the St. Petersburg foil. I was fortunate enough to win my second world cup in a row. I couldn't have dreamed of a better start of this Olympic season. It was only December 1991, and I was sure of a place on the Olympic team. But life can be tricky.

On the 20th of December, I was celebrating my birthday when the telephone rang. I picked it up. It was Alexander Perekalski. I thought: "How sweet, he wants to congratulate me!" But I was wrong, very wrong.

Perekalski was furious. He told me that my doping test in Vienna had been positive.

"What did you take?

"Nothing!"

"Your testosterone level is too high!"

What could I say? I was

> "You failed your drug test! Your testosterone is too high. *What were you taking?*"

innocent, but I didn't know where to turn. My results would be annulled. I would be banned from fencing for two years. No Olympic Games. Worse, what would I do? How would I earn a living? Fencing was all I knew. What was I without it?

According to protocol, a second sample now had to be analyzed. I had to pay $200.00 for the procedure. If the test was negative, I'd get my money back and go on with my fencing career. If it was positive, I'd lose my $200.00—a significant amount of money in that time and place—and worse, I'd be banned from fencing for two years.

In addition, a doctor could go to Germany to supervise the whole procedure, but I would have to pay for his plane ticket, his hotel, his visa, his pocket money. I figured that if I was "dirty" the first time, I would be dirty the second time too. So I decided not to pay for the doctor and his trip. I just paid $200.00 to Bazarevich, our FIE representative. All I could do was pray.

I kept telling Perekalski, "I didn't take anything. I didn't take anything"… I needed someone to believe me and have faith in me. Just a little while before, I had been having visions of fencing at the Olympics; now I was praying to God to clear my name.

In the end, I was cleared. After a very, very long three months, my case was closed. I could fence in the Olympics and my results still were in the world rankings.

So I kept on competing. I won the Tournament of Strongest for the third year in a row and fenced well in Venice, where I lost to Borella for first place. It was my third World Cup medal that season.

Then a black cat must have crossed my path. The Soviet team was beginning to have financial problems (there was no Soviet Union anymore) so we had to travel by bus to the World Cup in Budapest. On the way, I got sick. My fever kept me awake all night before the tournament. I went out after the first round with zero victories.

After I returned to Kiev, I still didn't feel well, but continued training. My father insisted that I go to the hospital for chest X-rays. I was diagnosed with pneumonia and immediately hospitalized.

This was the third time I had had pneumonia. My mother told me that I almost died of it at age five. Now, the doctors, looking at the X-rays, told me that I had the lungs of a forty-year-old smoker. That didn't make me feel any better.

My dad knew a doctor from that hospital who arranged to let me recover in the spinal injuries unit, rather than in the infectious diseases department. We both thought that I'd have a better chance of a quick recovery there. I was the only patient who could walk. The rest had different kinds of spinal fractures.

One of the patients in my ward was a burglar. He had almost been caught in the act of robbing an apartment. In the middle of his burglary, he heard a noise at the door—the owners were back! In a split second, he decided to leap from the balcony—not a brilliant idea. Fortunately, he landed in a tree and *only* broke his back—instead of killing himself. The amazing part of the story was that no one realized why he had jumped; otherwise, they would have called the police instead of the ambulance. He was lucky that way, but unlucky to break his back.

Another patient had an even dumber story. He and his friends went to a sauna, Russian style, drinking lots of vodka. He was feeling the sauna's heat and wanted to dive into the nearby swimming pool. He raced out into the night without turning the lights on. Whoops—no water! Another broken spine.

I got tons of antibiotics and dozen of injection every day…Three weeks later I won third place at the World Cup in Bonn.

The Olympics: Barcelona 1992

After my recovery, there were two months left until the Olympics in Barcelona. I fenced in a few tournaments and had couple training camps. My thoughts were about the Olympics; and about fencing in them.

I was also busy thinking about how not to get injured.)Once, my friend, the coach and former fencer Aleksandr Tikhomirov, told me a story.

Before a tournament, there was, as usual, a training camp. This one included football. One of the fencers objected:

"Do you think I am so that I'm going to risk injury before a key competition?"

While everyone else was playing, he did a few exercises and sat on the parallel bars, watching the game. When the game was over, he jumped down... and tore his knee ligaments. For the next two years, he was trying to recover from this injury.

What will be, will be.

Going into the games, I ranked first on the Soviet team—no, sorry, make that the Unified Team—along with Shevchenko, Mamedov, Ibragimov and Grigoriev. This would be the last time we would fence as a team together. This time, we would fence under the Olympic flag, not the Red flag, and as the Unified Team, not the USSR.

Romankov wasn't there. I still can't explain why. In January, at age 38, he won the Fabergé, a world cup event in Paris, and decided to go and coach in South Korea instead of trying to qualify for the Olympics. If he had been there, we might have taken a medal as a team. But it was his choice.

There was a poisonous atmosphere—not on our foil team, but among the sports bureaucracy. All the sports bosses, especially from the smaller republics, realized that they might never have a chance at an Olympic medal. They were making desperate deals to get their athletes onto the United Team: "Let my gymnast onto the team and I'll give up my fencer! Let my fencer onto the sabre team and I'll give up his spot in the individuals!" This was the last chance for the "Soviet Sports Machine."

The fencing team missed the opening ceremony of the Barcelona Olympics. We watched it on TV from Novogorsk. We got to Barcelona the next day.

The Barcelona Olympics was the biggest event and the most fascinating experience of my life, even though I have attended other Olympic Games since then.

Nevertheless, the living conditions were dreadful. Seven or eight athletes were crammed into each suite without air conditioning or a refrigerator. I shared a tiny room with Grigoriev and Shevchenko. It was so small that we had to store most of our stuff under our beds, and even then it spilled out into the living room.

On the other hand, the Olympic Village was right next to the sea. Everything was free—all kinds of food, refreshments, ice cream, bowling, a swimming pool all available almost 24/7...We joked that for a couple of weeks, we would finally be living in the communist paradise!

> In the Olympic Village, everything was free. Someone said, "Finally—the communist paradise!"

On the morning of the individual foil event, I woke up feeling nauseated and shaky. I forced myself to eat something and went to the fencing venue. After a thorough warm-up and the first few touches in the pools, I began to feel better. In the direct eliminations, I lost to the Pole Marian Sypniewski, but made it into the final through the "back door," by winning my way through the losers' bracket. I was a little tired, but had a couple of hours' window to rest up before the final of eight. I decided not to go to the Olympic Village and fell asleep on the chairs at the site. When I woke up, I couldn't even bend over to tie my shoes, and I had a pounding headache. The team doctor told me to take some aspirin, but after my doping scare, I was afraid to put any drug in my mouth. So I suffered throughout the final.

The final eight was really strong. Andrea Borella of Italy, Udo Wagner of Germany, Benny Wendt of Austria, Philippe Omnès of France, Elvis Gregory and Guillermo Betancourt of Cuba, Marian Sypniewski of Poland, and I would fight for Barcelona's gold.

In the quarterfinal, my first opponent was Betancourt. I gave him no chance, winning 5 – 1, 5 – 1. I felt that I was on a roll, storming him with flicks, showing no mercy. I should have felt great, but I had broken my favorite foil, the one I'd used all day; and my headache was so bad that I wished that someone would shoot me as soon as I stopped fencing.

In the semifinal, I had a very tense match with Elvis Gregory. I dropped the first bout 5 – 3. If I lost the next one, I'd be facing Udo Wagner in the third place bout. A loss to him would leave me without a medal, a prospect that didn't make me happy

The one minute break between bouts gave me a chance to reset my mind and my fencing. I had beaten Betancourt by speed; now I was trying to do the same against Elvis— but nobody then could ever be faster than Elvis Gregory! I needed to plan more carefully and try to outsmart my opponent by well-timed actions.

Elvis got up from the break with a charming smile on his face…

But I somehow found ways to win 5 – 2 and 5 – 1 and made it through to the final. I would be fencing Philippe Omnès of France. At that point I didn't care who I'd be fencing. I was so happy that I started crying uncontrollably. I couldn't

> I had made it to the Olympic final! I started crying uncontrollably.

stop. A huge load was off my shoulders. Thinking back on it, I guess I lost some energy and alertness at the same time. I was so delighted to be in the final of the Olympics that I was half-empty psychologically.

The memory of that final bout will stay with me, I guess, for the rest of my life. The last few touches haunted me in nightmares for years to come. They would play in my head over and over again, but always with the same ending.

I was strong, young and stupid. I had never lost to Omnès, and I would never lose to him again. But this bout—*for Olympic Gold!*—I lost.

The referee checked the foils. We touched each other's electric vests. I put my arm around Philippe's shoulder and wished him luck. I went back to the en-garde line and crossed myself. We saluted. The bout began.

In the first bout, I went out to a 3 – 1 lead, but Philippe came back to lead 4 – 3. I scored. 4 – 4. You had to win by two. He scored. 5 – 4. He made a long attack, but instead of finishing with a lunge, he simply ran off the side of the strip.

I burst out into laughter. I was out of control. It was so *stupid* of me! I should have attacked after that, but fenced defensively and got hit. First bout to Omnès.

I won the second bout 5 – 3 to even the score.

In the decisive bout, the score was tied 2 – 2. At that point, the referee, Andrea Magro, called my attack into preparation a counterattack, and I was behind 3 – 2 instead of leading. The next action was a simultaneous attack Philippe's light went on; mine didn't. There was an uninsulated wire was sticking out. I changed the weapon.

Now I was down 4 – 2. The referee's mistake and my weapon's malfunction had left me in a deep hole. What I needed to do was concentrate, refocus, get a second wind. But I didn't know how. The situation had developed too quickly for me to handle. I lost my control, and the bout, 5 – 2.

I was furious with myself. It was a good ten minutes before the tournament organizers could get me to come out for the awarding of the medals.

But when I came back, there was a very special moment. The Unified Team, representing the republics of the former USSR, had a flag, which was carried at the opening and closing ceremonies and was raised for its teams. But when an individual won a medal, it would be the flag of his or her republic that fluttered to the top of the flagpole.

Our Ukrainian Parliament had voted to change the red and blue flag of the Ukrainian Soviet Socialist Republic into the yellow and blue flag of newly independent Ukraine. Standing on the podium, I saw my country's new flag raised for the very first time.

I wasn't satisfied with my personal result (of course not, how could I be?), but I was fiercely proud for my country.

> I wasn't satisfied for myself, but I was still proud, and I was *fiercely* proud for my country.

I would have been even more furious with myself than I was if I had realized that this was my best chance I would ever have to win Olympic gold. Now I know that…Even now, years later, the younger generation is still sure that I sold that bout for money

I didn't sell that bout; I blew it. It's that simple.

After the awards ceremony, I went back to the Olympic Village and phoned my dad with the news. A Silver Medal in the Olympics—it was beginning to sound good to me.

But my father only said: "Why second?" I felt let down and a little bitter. Only now can I understand his reaction. My father is a maximalist—he wants it all. I am a maximalist too. I guess I get it from him. For both of us, there is only one place worth having—first.

There was prize money from the Olympic Committee of the CIS. I got $2000, and Perekalski and my father shared

$2000. Of course, I was still a little worried about my doping test. But after two days I had heard nothing about it and figured that the medal was mine to keep

The Barcelona Olympics followed an unwritten motto, "Everyone is playing fair; everyone is clean." Barcelona was the home town of Juan Antonio Samaranch, the head of the Olympic movement at the time. No one wanted to spoil his party.

One track and field athlete won a medal there, but was hanging his head the day after the event when I met him in the Village.

"What's the matter?" I asked.

"I'm dirty and I know it," he said. "I'm going to have my medal taken away and be barred from my sport."

I met him in the Village a few days later, and he had a big smile on his face. He was going to keep his medal and be able to compete on the professional Grand Prix track and field circuit. Even though he knew he was "dirty," the lab had declared him "clean."

In the team event, we thought we had a good shot at the Gold Medal. The first day we fenced well, beating France in the qualification round. I won all four of my bouts, taking a very unsatisfactory "revenge" on Omnès. The next day, in the quarters, we met Poland. We were sure of our victory…too sure. The Polish fencers had another opinion. I lost two bouts out of 4, which wasn't good at all. We lost to Poland, won a couple of other matches, and finished in fifth place.

Afterwards, Shevchenko, Grigoriev and I sat in the Village crying as if someone had died. Our hopes for medals had died, but even worse, our team had died. The Soviet Foil Team breathed its last in 1992, in Barcelona.

Some of us had futures in

> Afterwards, we sat in the Olympic Village crying as if someone had died. The Soviet Team had died in 1992, in Barcelona.

team foil. Mamedov and Ibragimov were already Olympic Foil Team Champions from Seoul '88. Shevchenko and Mamedov would become Olympic Foil Team Champions (for Russia) in Atlanta '96, four years later.

Well done, guys! Cheers!

I won another prize in Barcelona, one that surprised me at the time. I had been so wrapped up in making the Soviet Olympic Team that I hadn't been following the overall World Cup standings. I was riding the shuttle bus from the Olympic Village to the fencing venue one day, I found myself next to Jochen Behr, one of the chiefs of the German foil team, who was shuffling through some papers.

After a few moments, he looked up. "Congratulations!" he said. "You won the World Cup."

I thought he must be kidding me, but he showed the rankings. The good news did a lot to ease my disappointments. I was number one in the world! Number One, with Olympic silver on my neck. I could live with that.

There are so many memories from those Games that I could share with you, some happy, some sad.

It's always sad when a teammate loses out on a chance for the gold medal. There's always a little drama behind each story. I could tell a lot of stories like that, but I'd rather tell a pleasant one.

We were in sitting in a sort of bar for the athletes, right next to the fencing venue, watching the epee final on TV, right next to the fencing hall. We had finished competing and could enjoy a beer and unwind. It tasted even better, because it was free.

Suddenly, our sabre teammate Georgi Pogosov walked in. He said that Hollywood actors were watching the final at the fencing site—famous actors—Michael Douglas and Jack Nicholson!

Maybe the fencers didn't believe him, but nobody seemed too excited by this news. For my part, I jumped off my chair and headed for the fencing hall.

It was true! There they were, enjoying the fencing. Immediately, I decided that I was going to get Nicholson's autograph. I had seen him in "One Flew Over the Cuckoo's Nest" and his performance as the independent-minded rebel McMurphy had excited me.

Nicholson and Douglas were watching in the stands reserved for spectators (we athletes had our own separate stands). I don't remember what I told the site personnel, but I made my way into the spectator stands and found a free seat four rows above my intended victim. But how to reach him?

I was sitting next to some big guy who was talking in Italian on a walky-talky. I looked around and noticed quite a few "big guys" sitting around the actors. Bodyguards!

I asked my neighbor, if it was possible to get Jack Nicholson's autograph. He looked me over, then talked to someone on the walky-talky. While he was talking, I noticed, that almost everyone in the stands had a pen and a piece of paper in their hands. They weren't watching the final, but waiting for a possibility to get autographs. "Go downstairs and ask that man", the bodyguard told me, pointing with his finger. I followed instructions. The guy turned and spoke to the actors.

Michael Douglas looked at me questioningly. I gestured to him: just sit back, man, I don't need you, I need Jack!

Nicholson looked at me, and said: "No!"

I had to find the right words as fast as possible. I said to the bodyguard: "Could you tell Mr. Nicholson, that I'm a silver medalist at these Olympics and also the World Cup winner!" And again, he turned to Jack and spoke Nicholson looked at me again and nodded OK.

I didn't have a pen, I didn't have paper. Somebody gave me a pen. I took my accreditation card and passed it to Nicholson, with the words: "My name is Sergei". I wasn't sure, if he heard me.

I got my card back. On the ticket (which gave us right to use public transport free), I read: "To Sergei with regards—Jack Nicholson.".

Was that cool or what?

A few minutes later they left the fencing venue. No one else got an autograph.

Personally, I prefer the Olympic closing ceremony to the opening. It's not so formal; you don't have to spend hours on your feet; you can sit in the stands and enjoy the show.

It was great to see and hear the best tenors of the world, but it was very sad to listen to Montserrat Caballé singing the song "Barcelona" without Freddie Mercury...

These Olympics divided the lives of all the athletes of the former USSR into a simple Before and After. After these Games I had to make my own way without the support of a powerful team. Fencing for Ukraine, I would know that I would only have one chance for a medal—individually. It felt as if I had to start a new life, with new objectives and goals. It wasn't easy. Trust me on that. I had invested a lot in a USSR foil team that no longer existed. It's difficult to describe what I felt then, but I knew that I had to regroup.

After the Olympics, I returned to Kiev and relaxed for a week. There were parties and receptions. The Ukrainians on the United Team met with the President of Ukraine.

A few days later, I got married. I was a few months short of twenty-three years old.

Doping: The Sword of Damocles

1992—1993

I began the new season by taking second place at a World Cup in St. Petersburg, losing to Cerioni in the final by a few touches.

During the Barcelona Olympics, the FIE had elected a new president, René Roch. There was grave concern at that time that fencing would be dropped from the Olympics. One of the reasons was that fencing was not thought to be a true world sport. At that time, there were only a few World Cups scattered throughout the fencing season, so they were only held in a few countries. Under Roch, the number of World Cups increased dramatically, and they were held throughout the world.

> Under FIE President René Roch, there were many more World Cups and they were held throughout the world.

Early in 1993, I was invited to fence in Zurich in a Candidate A tournament. The winner would get about 5000 Swiss Francs, about $3000.00—a lot of money from a Ukrainian point of view! I won the tournament, beating Thorsten Weidner in the semis and Stefano Cerioni in the final, but the shadow of suspicion still followed me. The tournament organizer told me that I would get my prize only after the results of the doping control were known. He said he'd be at the Venice World Cup, only two weeks away, and let me know the results of the analysis.

Obviously, I was going to go to Venice.

This created a problem. Italy didn't have an embassy in Ukraine yet. Instead of training, I had to go to Moscow for my visa. I didn't have the money to fly to Moscow, so I spent three days and nights on the train traveling to Moscow and back. Then the Ukrainian Fencing Federation didn't have the money to fly me to Venice. So I had to travel 2,000 kilometers, again by train, alone.

The route was Kiev—Budapest—Venice. I got my ticket from the Ukraine Sports Committee, but I didn't have any idea about the exact route or what countries I'd be traveling through.

These days, you can travel everywhere in Europe on a single visa. At that time, however, I needed a visa for every country the train was going to pass through. I got to Budapest without incident, then boarded the "Gondolier" for Venice.

There were two possible routes. The first passed through Croatia and Slovenia. For this, I didn't need an extra visa, because both countries were part of the former Yugoslavia and had a no-visa arrangement with the former USSR. But the second route would pass through Austria, and for this I would need a visa—which I didn't have, because I was certain that the train would take the no-visa route. Surely the Sports Committee had booked me on the right itinerary!

You can see where this story is going. There I was in my compartment, getting ready for the thirteen-hour ride from Budapest to Venice. The train pulled out of Budapest and shortly later stopped at a station.

The sign read VIENNA. I was in Austria! I began to panic.

I didn't have a visa! I'd be arrested! They'd never let me through without a visa! I wouldn't fence in the tournament!

The committee wouldn't give me my money back for the ticket! (Ukraine was so short of money that I had to finish in the top three just to get reimbursed.)

There was a knock on the door of my compartment, and the customs policeman came in. He started to look for my visa. I just told him that I didn't have one. He gave me a long, hard look.

Desperately, I showed him some magazines from the Barcelona Olympics with my picture in them. He skimmed through them.

"So what?" he said.

"I'm an athlete," I said. "I'm traveling from Budapest to Venice on a ticket that my federation bought for me. I had no idea that I would be going through Austria. If I don't fence, I'll have thrown my money away. Please, just le me go through."

He gave me that stare again. There was a pause.

Then he said, "OK! Just don't make this mistake again!"

I almost collapsed in relief...until I realized that I'd have to go through another passport control before Italy. I stayed nervous for the next ten hours.

The border police came again. I repeated my monologue.

"OK! Just don't make this mistake again!"

What had worked—my picture in the magazine or just my saying "please?" I was left wondering about that—and about how I was going to handle the return trip along the same route! (In fact, I straightened things out at the Austrian consulate in Venice and had no more trouble of that kind.)

But trouble was waiting for me in Venice. The next day, as I entered the fencing venue, I could see all the Italian and German fencers staring at me knew immediately that something was very wrong.

A Swiss official in a suit came up to me with a nasty little smile on his face.

"I'm sorry, Mr. Golubitsky," he said. "I'm going to have to take your prize money back. Your drug test was positive. You have too much testosterone, Mr. Golubitsky!"

I handed the check over. My world was crumbling. I hadn't taken anything illegal — ever, but all my fellow fencers were going to think that I had won because I cheated.

The ancient Damocles had a sword suspended over his head by a single thread. That was how I felt.

At least I was allowed to fence in Venice. I took third place in that tournament, losing to Udo Wagner. He just killed me, 5 – 1, 5 – 0. Almost immediately, I started hearing the rumors: I had thrown the match, taking money from the German in exchange for his easy win.

Whatever I did looked bad these days. If I won, it was because of drugs; if I lost, I had thrown the bout. It was all so unfair.

The Ukrainian Fencing Federation reimbursed me for my trip (my third place at least ensured that), but I was going to have to do something about this new doping charge. I had to clear my name and claim my prize money, which after all I had won fair and square.

I wrote a strong letter to René Roch, the President of the FIE. I told him that I had never used drugs. I added that Ukraine was in a very difficult economic situation, and that the 5000 Swiss Francs (US $3,000.00) was big money to me, especially considering that my salary at that time was only about US $200.00 per month!

It would take me another year to clear my name. Finally, in 1994, the FIE let me decide where I'd like to be tested: Ukraine or Paris. I chose Paris, because I could fence for prize money there, and two weeks later, compete in the Fabergé World Cup. I took third in the Bourg-la-Reine tournament, losing in the semis to Lionel Plumenail of France, the future Silver Medalist in the 1996 Olympics. Immediately after, I went to the clinic for the crucial test.

Medical vampires drained my blood and checked my urine...and to my immense relieve, cleared me: they established that my natural level of testosterone was higher than the doping control allowed for. The Swiss had to give me my prize money back. But for the whole next year, after each World Cup, whether I had finished first or last, I was likely to have to undergo a doping test.

I was left with a week to see the sights of Paris before the Fabergé World Cup. I had a great time. The sword of doping was no longer hanging over my head.

If it wasn't one thing, it was another. A few days before the competition, something I ate seriously disagreed with me. Maybe it was the oysters. I got a massive stomach ache and spent most of my time in the bathroom. So I went to a pharmacy.

I said to the manager, "I'm an international athlete. I have a competition in a few days. Be careful what you give me!"

I took the medicine for a few days...then read the fine print on the label. Oh, my God! *Extract of opium!* First testosterone...now opium!

More medical advice: "Drink beer, 24/7! Wash it out of your system!"

Under the circumstances, I wasn't thinking about a high result at the tournament. The only thing I was concentrating on was to get out of there as quickly as possible. I lost in the round of 32, hailed a taxi to the airport. The last thing I heard before leaving Coubertin Hall was, "Mr. Golubitsky, please proceed to doping control." Fortunately, I hadn't signed any paper that would oblige me to undergo doping control at this tournament, so I couldn't be disqualified.

The moral of the story: Don't be an idiot! Check the ingredients of any medicine you are taking—it's your responsibility!

I Get the Girl

During the 1992-93 season, I won only one World Cup Tournament, the "Lion of Bonn." My wife Liudmila was in her fifth month of pregnancy. We had decided to travel together and have some fun in Germany.

The day before the competition, the organizers held a fencing gala in Petersberg Castle, which must be one of the most beautiful places in the world—a splendid luxury hotel built on the site of an 800-year-old monastery overlooking the River Rhine as if from an airplane. The hero Siegfried slew the dragon in these hills, and heads of state held conferences and signed treaties here in the hotel. Liudmila and I were treated like royalty. I felt important and famous, which doesn't happen that often in a fencer's career. On top of all that, we had the use of a Mercedes for three days!

At the gala, four of us—Philippe Omnès, Uli Schreck, Udo Wagner, and I—fenced the semi-finals and finals before a distinguished black-tie crowd. The occasion excited me. I think that fencing is more than a sport: it is a show, a spectacle, and that we as fencers have to play our roles in order to make the spectators love our sport and have fun watching it. Before the bouts started, I turned to the Master of Ceremonies, a well-known German TV sportscaster.

"You know," I told him, "It really wouldn't be bad to have a beer right now."

"No problem," he said.

I made the final of the gala and was getting ready to fence Omnès for first place. We went onto the strip in the huge hall, in front of the distinguished crowd, in the silence of the huge hall. Suddenly, I turned to the host.

"You'll never become Chancellor of Germany," I told him. "You don't keep your promises!"

He motioned to a waiter. In a moment, Omnès, the host and I all had steins of beer in our hands. Still on the strip, we toasted each other, drank the beer, saluted, and began fencing.

Two days later, I beat Philippe Omnès "for real"—in the finals of the Lion of Bonn. The German newspapers were full of stories about me taking revenge on Philippe for Barcelona. Frankly, I would rather have beaten Philippe in the Olympic final, even if it had meant losing to him in every bout for the rest of my life.

Meanwhile, the World Championships were approaching. I wanted to get ready for the Championships (which would be held in Essen, Germany) and to get Liudmila away from Kiev as much as possible, I didn't think that Kiev was such a great place to be after the disaster of 1986, when the Chernobyl nuclear reactor exploded less than a hundred miles away. I got my chance to kill two birds with one stone: when Lazar Adirim, the Israeli head coach, invited me to prepare in Israel with the Israeli National Team. I got permission from my father (in his role as my coach) and went, accompanied by Liudmila. It was our first visit to the land of Jesus, and we had a wonderful time, going on excursions to Jerusalem and many holy places.

I was obsessed with the idea of having a baby boy, a son who would carry on the Golubitsky name. In Israel, we had a chance to have a scan done and to look for the first time at our future child. At the clinic, I didn't go with Liudmila and the doctor. I'm superstitious: I thought that if I didn't look, the baby would be sure to be a boy.

Time passed. My wife came into the room with a broad smile.

I looked at her: "Well?"

"It's not 100% sure, but it looks like it's…a girl."

I wanted a second opinion.

The next day, we went to a different clinic, with a different doctor. This time I went in also.

And the doctor showed me: "Look, there's one leg, there's another leg—but there's no third leg!"

I wasn't delighted, but I wasn't unhappy either.

After training hard *and* having a good time for a change, I returned to Kiev feeling strong and ready for the World Championships. My father was head coach of the national team. For the first time, my father would be with me for this most important tournament of the season.

Nasty rumors swirled around me on my arrival in Essen. The Italian epeeist Angelo Mazzoni was saying that I had sold my bout to Omnès at the '92 Olympics, and soon enough I heard about it. Mazzoni was a great fencer, so of course I knew his name, but I had never spoken with him. I didn't get it—why would he slander me when he didn't know anything at all about the subject?

It didn't take me long to find Mazzoni. I walked up to him and introduced myself.

"What's going on?" I asked him. "Why are you saying things like that about me?"

"I was talking to some sportswriters," he said, "and they were asking me about the time I myself was accused of throwing a bout."

"So?"

"So I got mad at them. I told them, 'You shouldn't be talking to me; you should be talking to Golubitsky—he's the one who sells bouts, not me."

"Next time, mind your own business," I said.

We shook hands on it.

I had a superstition at that time: I never gave autographs before an event. I thought it would jinx me. There was one German collector who was after me day and night.

I told him, "Look, I'll give you all the autographs you want, but not before the Championships." But he kept after me.

I was talking to the British fencer Johnny Davies when the collector came up to me. I had a sudden flash. I told him that Davies was my manager and that I couldn't sign any cards without his permission. As the collector turned to Johnny, I gave him a signal: play along.

"No problem," he told the collector. "But it will cost you 10 Deutsche Marks [about $6.00] per autograph."

"That's too much," said the collector. "I can pay you 5 DM."

Johnny and I cracked up. The whole thing had been a joke.

In the tournament, I beat Uwe Roemer in the semifinal and faced off against Alex Koch in the final. The format at that time was best of three bouts, and you had to win by two touches. In no time, I was down 4 – 2 in the first bout. I couldn't find the right time for my actions and my fencing was out of sync. My father told me that under some circumstances, it's better to let a bout go in order to prepare yourself mentally for the next one. That's what I was doing—literally walking up to him with my legs straight. But for some reason, the plan to throw the bout didn't work. I made some great actions and caught up with him: 3 – 4, 4 – 4, 5 – 4 my favor. In the end, Alex and I attacked simultaneously—and he missed! My bout! I couldn't believe that I had stolen the first bout.

> Sometimes it's better to let a bout go in order to prepare yourself mentally for the next one. That's what I was trying to do—but my opponent wouldn't let me!

Alex won the second bout, 5 – 2. The third bout would be decisive.

With the score 2 – 2, I made an attack on Alex's preparation. The referee, Andrea Magro, blew the call, just as he had done in the final bout in Barcelona (no hard feelings, Andrea!), calling it my counterattack. Instead of winning 3 – 2, I was losing 3 – 2. I blew my cool, losing my rhythm and the bout, 5 – 2.

It was a replay of the Barcelona final. For the second year in a row, I had won the overall World Cup, but once again finished second in the big event.

And I started hearing the whispers again. Even some of the chiefs of my own Ukrainian team were saying that I had sold the bout.

It wasn't until years later that I figured out why rumors like this always followed me. During important bouts, even at the Olympics or World Championships, I always fenced with a smile on my face. Why not? I was having fun, and I was trying to entertain the spectators too. Maybe I looked as if I was having too much fun. So if I won, people would say I was the greatest, but if I lost, I must have thrown the bout. From 1992 on, my *best* fencing was at such a high level that people just didn't believe I could lose if I didn't want to. It was a compliment, in a way.

But it wasn't true at all. I knew why I lost. I still didn't know how to win *when I had to*. World Cup events are important, of course. But the overall World Cup championship depends on a cumulative result. It's not so bad to lose in a World Cup, and you gain respect and standing by winning. If you finish second, or sixteenth, one week, there will be another event a few weeks later.

The World Championships are entirely different. You win or you don't. You have to show what you can do right then and there. There is no next week.

For two seasons now, I couldn't take that last, decisive step. I had lost in close bouts. I couldn't stay focused, even when I needed to the most. I still had the attitude that I had plenty of time; I'd win sooner or later. I didn't understand that every tournament I fenced might be the last one of my career.

I was immature. I was twenty-three years old.

A week later, in Buffalo, New York, I took "revenge" on Alex, beating him 5 – 3, 5 – 3 for first place in the World

University Games. It's a prestigious event in the world of fencing; most of the world's best fencers take part. I was at the top of my game that week, feeling almost as if I was an adult fencing against children.

Two great fencers shared third place, Alessandro Puccini and Lionel Plumenail. I stood on the highest place on the podium, with them and Alex on the lower spots… and I was almost crying with frustration. I had taken another meaningless revenge instead of getting the job done a week earlier.

I got the chance to fence epee there. Ukraine had only four epeeists instead of five: the usual financial problems. I was the reserve.

During the match with Kazakhstan, Maxim Paramonov got injured and I had to fence for him. I had to fence my former teammate, Slava Grigoriev (Kazakhstan had even worse financial problems than Ukraine—they had *two* foilists fencing epee and *no* reserves.)

Not surprisingly, my bout with Grigoriev was full of foil actions. We reached 4 – 4 in a messy struggle. I really wanted to win, but at the same time, I wanted to make a good "epee touch." The result was beautiful.

I feinted toward his foot. Recognizing the feint, he pretended to parry. Then I disengaged and threatened his foot again. This time he *had* to parry. In doing so, he opened his wrist for a shot from above—exactly what I was waiting for! I hit him: 5 – 4!

We won that match and had to fence the Hungarian team. I went three for three. Not bad for a foil fencer, huh?

Buffalo, New York, is a center for Ukrainian immigrants, and for me, this was the best part of this University Games. Almost for the first time in my life, I could hear my native Ukrainian language in its original form. In my own country, the language is full of Russian words and expressions, which is only logical, because we were under Russian domination for so long.

After the individual final, I was privileged to be invited

to have dinner with a Ukrainian family. They gave me a gift: an 1889 silver dollar, which I still keep for good luck.

Overall, the season had been good for me. I had won silver in the World Championships to go with gold in the overall World Cup and gold in the World University Games. On top of that, I graduated from the University of Kiev with a degree as a fencing coach. My family and I could take pride in these achievements, even if I privately thought I could do better.

The overall World Cup championship had to mean something, right? When I got back to Kiev, I was invited to a press conference and was told that I had been selected as Ukrainian athlete of the month. An interview was set up with Kiev's biggest newspaper.

A few days later I read that a football (soccer) player had been named to that honor. He had scored a couple of goals in the final of the *Ukrainian* championship. So my *world* results didn't count against his *national* results...in soccer. I will never get tired of saying that it's better to be number one in the world in fencing, than number 36 in some popular commercial sport. What do you think?

But I had to admit: I would have had a better case if I'd been World Champion.

1993—1994

I rested for a few weeks and started over again. My preparation began at a camp in Alushta, in the Crimea. It was the camp from hell. I had gained a few kilos during the break following the World Championships, and I had to lose them. Even a few extra kilos make a big difference to an fencer. You're carrying them around all day, as if they were in your back pack. You get tired much faster and you're more likely to be injured.

Then I got sick. It was a combination of food poisoning and a strain in my Achilles tendon. Plus my back was hurting. This is the price you pay for being overweight.

Over the course of the following week, I fenced 65 five-touch bouts and sixteen 15-touch bouts. It felt like "Rocky:" I was punching the meat carcasses and running up the Art Museum steps. "No pain!"

It was all in preparation for the European Championships in Linz, Austria.

Meanwhile, according to the doctors, Liudmila had two or two and a half weeks before the baby was due. I went to Linz thinking that: believing that I'd have plenty of time to get back to Kiev before the baby was born.

It was a hard trip. It took us 40 hours by train to get from Kiev to Linz. I was really tired and didn't fence well at all. Somewhere in Direct Elimination I found myself behind, 13 – 4, to my friend Benny Wendt. It was too much.

Then another 40 hours back to Kiev. I checked in with my mother by telephone.

"Hi, Mom."

"Hello…Daddy."

Daddy? I couldn't believe what I was hearing. My face was covered with tears. I couldn't understand the words I was hearing. Finally, my mother got through to me.

"Everything is fine.

Liudmila is fine.

Your baby girl is fine."

"Your wife is fine. Your baby girl is fine."

I felt that I was flying.

Tears were running down my face. I couldn't speak. I felt that I was flying.

I took a taxi from the railroad station to the student hostel where Liudmila and I were living (there was no way

159

I could afford an apartment, but we wanted a place of our own). I picked up my car and drove immediately to the hospital.

Liudmila showed me my daughter through the window of the newborns' ward. She had a red face and a lot of black hair on her head. She was tall — 54 cm. long — and she weighed 3.9 kg. She really wasn't beautiful then.

"Sorry, sweetheart!" I whispered to her through the glass.

We named her Elena, in honor of Liudmila's mom. For three weeks, I was celebrating Elena's birth with parties and family gatherings.

With My Daughter, Elena

The World Cup Years

For a while after Elena's birth I hardly trained at all. After that, for the whole rest of the season, I had a lot of sleepless nights trying to hold Liudmila with the baby. There was no way I could practice properly.

On top of those disruptions, the year's first World Cup, in Vienna, involved a thirty-three hour train ride.

This was the first World Cup to employ the new system that is still in use as I write this. The top sixteen fencers by world ranking get byes on the first day of the tournament. Everybody else has to fence for the remaining forty-eight spots in the tableau of sixty-four. On the main day, the format is direct elimination with no repechage (losers' bracket) from sixty-four to the final eight. The final eight, generally held after a break, is also direct elimination.

In one way, the old system was fairer: there were three rounds of pools leading to a tableau of 32 with repechage to the final of eight. (Still earlier, there had been a final pool of six in which everyone fenced everyone else.) In the older systems, the winner would actually be the best fencer, with little chance of a fluke resulting from the luck of the draw.

On the other hand, under the old system there had been far too many deals between fencers, which was against the spirit of fair play. I've told you about some of these.

In addition, the new system is much more predictable in its timing, so it's better for TV—and therefore for the sport as a whole.

The problem with it is that there's no room for error. You lose, you're out.

I guess that takes us back to the original spirit of the duel!

In Vienna, I was seeded first, so I didn't have to fence the first day. That was fine for me, considering the shape I was in. The next day I beat Thomas Endres, Anvar Ibragimov, and Alessandro Puccini on the way to the final. For first place, I squeaked past Udo Wagner 15 – 14, and after another thirty-three hours on the train, I could enjoy my first victory of the new season.

Three weeks later, after a 24-hour train ride with the team, I arrived at St. Petersburg for another World Cup.

I'm not proud of what happened the night before the competition, but it's part of my story. I ran into my friend, the Israeli head coach Lazar Adirim, whom I hadn't seen since the last World Championships. We drank a toast to friendship. Then, of course, we drank to my daughter. We started with wine, then vodka, champagne, whiskey, and some sweet liqueur I don't recall the name of. We drank all night. I slept just two hours before the competition.

I shambled into the fencing hall exuding a thick fog of alcoholic vapors. There was no way I could warm up: I would have puked. How was I going to fence?

Very effectively, as it happened! No one scored more than ten touches on me until I meet Puccini in the final. I beat him 15 – 13 for my second World Cup in a row.

Readers: Do not imitate this foolish behavior! Don't use this episode as a precedent! I deserved to lose that tournament. I was just as dumb then as I had been when I took that medication in Paris the year before.

Zurich was the scene of the next cup. Once again, I had a bye in the first round, so I didn't have to fence the first day. But I was beginning to notice something: the guys who fenced and survived Day One were meaner and hungrier on Day Two. They were more tired physically, but mentally better prepared to fight.

To meet their challenge, I had to change my preparation. While the first day's fencing was going on, I was out on the track, doing a half hour of running and some stretching. At Zurich, the track was next to the fencing hall, and I could see the wondering glances of the coaches and fencers. I guess that in their opinion, I should be taking the day off and relaxing. But next day, in the finals, I beat Alex Koch 15 – 13 to win my third consecutive World Cup title that year.

A new "Italian adventure" awaited me in Venice. By now, an Italian consulate had opened in Kiev, but they hadn't officially started to issue visas yet. If you were a Very Important Person, the consulate would issue a visa; ordinary citizens still had to go to Moscow. Grigori Kriss got me an audience. To my surprise, I found myself talking about fencing. The consul even knew my name as well as those of many other fencers. He told me that even though the consulate didn't issue visas yet, he'd be glad to write an official letter that would let me enter Italy, sparing me the waste of several days traveling to Moscow and back. This time, too, the Ukrainian Fencing Federation agreed to support my travel to the extent of $300.00 toward an airline ticket. The rest of my expenses would be up to me. The least expensive flight from Kiev to Venice went through Moscow. I telephoned Ilgar Mamedov and asked him to help me reserve the ticket. The price was exactly what my fencing federation had budgeted: I'd be paying (in rubles) the equivalent of 300 bucks.

As you may remember, I had been a member of the Soviet KGB, which was now the Security Service of Ukraine, the SBU. I was a lieutenant, and I was permitted to carry a gun. I had no reason to carry my ID outside of

Ukraine, but I was carrying it this time.

The day I got to Moscow, the Russian ruble dropped in value. Now I was going to have to come up with the equivalent of an extra $50.00 in rubles out of my own pocket.

Right outside the exchange office, a women with a Ukrainian accent came up to me. She offered to sell me rubles on the black market—at a much better exchange rate, exactly $50.00 better, in fact. I gave her my dollars, got her rubles…and barely had time to say thanks when I felt a hand on my shoulder. I turned and faced the red ID of a Russian policeman. I was under arrest for "illegal operations with foreign currency." They arrested the woman, too.

I didn't think they'd put me in jail, which would have been a major disaster. I thought that they'd much rather take all my money and let me go, which would have been a much smaller disaster, but a disaster nonetheless. So I showed them my SBU ID.

"Look," I said. "We're colleagues, kind of."

I wouldn't have been surprised if they didn't care at all. Many Russians didn't think much of Ukrainian independence. But in the end, they let me go.

Probably they got the money from the Ukrainian woman instead.

This wasn't the end of my troubles. The next morning, Ilgar took me to Moscow's Sheremetievo Airport. I asked him to stick with me until I cleared security, customs, and passport control.

"Don't worry," he said. "I've used the same kind of consular letter many times without a visa. It always works."

He wished me good luck and headed back to Moscow.

No sooner was he gone than I ran into trouble at the Aeroflot check-in desk. The letter was no good; they wanted a visa if I was going to fly. For thirty minutes I was talking, begging, explaining, but all to no avail. Finally they called someone higher up.

My spirits rose when I saw him. He had a Dinamo pin on his lapel. I said to myself, this is my guy!

I told him my story. Then he told me his.

The problem was that if the Italians sent me back for flying without a visa. Aeroflot would have to pay a hefty fine. Would I pay the fine if this happened? Sure, I said, without a moment's hesitation, and he signaled to security to let me through.

Well, the Italians didn't give me any trouble at passport control.

And once in Venice, I fought my way to the finals, where I met Uwe Roemer. I looked hard into his eyes before the bout started. He looked hard back at me, and I knew I was in for trouble. Every touch was a struggle, but finally victory was mine, 15 – 13.

> I looked into his eyes. From the way he looked back at me, I knew I was in for troubfe. Every touch was a struggle, but victory was finally mine.

In addition, I won a World Cup in Budapest that year.

I had won five World Cups. The last one of the season was in Paris. The French sports daily, *L'Equipe,* saluted me with the nickname, "Sergei the Terrible" and an article titled, "Everyone Against Golubitsky," urging someone to come forward and stop me. But it didn't happen. I beat Dmitri Shevchenko in the semis and Laurent Bel of France in the final.

During the 1993-'94 season, I had fenced in eight World Cup tournaments and won six. I had high hopes for the World Championships in Athens. The event would take place in the same venue where I had fenced my last international junior event.

Giovanna Trillini of Italy was also having a great season, having won six of nine world cups. There was a big story on the sports pages with our pictures. The headline read,

"The Devil's Two Blades." Obviously, we were favorites. But somebody upstairs had other plans. We didn't win.

In fact, even though I was the number one seed, I didn't even make it to the final eight.

I didn't have to fence my first bout in the tableau of 64 because my opponent failed to show up. I won my next and was waiting to fence the winner of the match between my compatriot Samoilov and Dong of China. With a tremendous effort, Dong won, 15 – 13.

I had never seen the Chinese fencer before. How strong could he be, if he almost lost to my teammate? I made the huge mistake of underestimating my opponent.

I was behind the whole bout. Dong held a three-touch advantage all the way to 14 – 11. I fought back to make the score 14 – 13.

I attacked with a feint. Dong tried to parry, but I made a last-moment disengage and lunge to tie the score 14 – 14. Or so I thought. Dong had never touched my blade with his parry, but he *had* whacked my knee, making a sound so loud that everyone heard it. The referee mistook the sound for Dong's parry and gave him the riposte and the bout. In vain did I show him my bleeding knee. The decision stood and I was out.

> The defeat taught me a lesson: I would never again take any opponent too lightly.

This defeat taught me a lesson: for the rest of my life, I would never take an opponent too lightly.

The Cuban Rolando Tucker won that World Championship, to the surprise of most of the experts.

Giovanna Trillini also went down. I saw her crying after her defeat. I felt her pain as if it had been mine. The only thing I could offer was a hug.

At least I was sure I had won the overall World Cup. But not so fast...Alessandro Puccini's second place finish at the World Championships, combined with my debacle, put tied Puccini and me on points. In the end, though, I won the overall World Cup because I had won more World Cup events.

The following year, the FIE changed the system. From then on, the World Championships and the World Cup were completely separate. World Championship results would no longer count toward the World Cup title.

This was my third overall World Cup title in a row… with no medal in a major.

1994—1995

1994 — '95 would be another great year for me, but it didn't start brilliantly. It opened with the European championships in Krakow, Poland. I decided to repeat my experiment from St. Petersburg the year before. The night before the competition, I got drunk. This time I was decisively punished for my stupidity. Ilgar Mamedov spanked me, 15 – 3, in the round of 16. I finished ninth.

Afterwards, Liudmila came to Krakow with our daughter. For many years, my friend Grzegorz Agata had organized an annual gala tournament, "Poland vs. the World." Over the course of the years, I have had the honor of fencing for the World team with Philippe Omnès, Alexander Koch, Dmitri Shevchenko, Benny Wendt, Stefano Cerioni, Lionel Plumenail, and Thorsten Weidner. It was always a fine event: an occasion to make new friends and cement old friendships.

This year was extra special. My daughter Elena was baptized in the Catholic church of the little town of Pabianice. Grzegorz Agata became her godfather.

My World Cup season opened with a victory in Vienna. Next came St. Petersburg, where in the semis I faced Stefano Cerioni of Italy.

I had a big lead, 13 – 7, late in the third and final period. I asked the timekeeper how much time was left.

"Seven seconds," she told me.

Stefano had a reputation as an aggressive and temperamental fencer. Every so often, he would get a black card and be disqualified for his behavior. I actually saw him give the finger to a referee after he had lost a bout in the quarters. He is a tall, strongly built man, who often gave hard touches.

I decided to avoid the risk of pain. On *"Allez!"* (the command to fence), I stepped backward, and backward... and off the strip. I knew I'd be penalized a touch, but with a 13 – 7 lead, I didn't care.

I didn't expect Stefano's reaction. He walked up to me.

"Attenzione! (Watch out!)" he growled. He thought I was making fun of him.

I tried to calm him down and we got ready to continue the match. This time, as soon as the referee said *"Allez!"* the buzzer went off to signal that the bout was over. Stefano and I shook hands. He looked puzzled.

I asked him why he was upset. He told me. At the same moment I asked the timekeeper how much time was left in the bout, he was asking his trainer—and being told that there was *a minute* and seven seconds to go. Ouch!

> At the moment I was asking the timekeeper how much time was left, he was asking his trainer.

In the final, I beat Laurent Bel for my second World Cup victory of the season.

January saw three World Cup competitions. In Havana, I took second, losing to Rolando Tucker. I won in Zurich for the third year in a row and finished fifth in Paris. The next tournament would be in Venice, the scene of my repeated travel problems.

Once again, along with Samoilov, I had to travel by train. This time the federation bought the right tickets, routing us through Croatia and Slovenia. The trip took 45 hours, and we arrived in Venice exhausted. I reached the quarter finals, but couldn't do anything with Shevchenko and lost 15 – 6.

After Venice, the Circolo Scherma Fides (Fides Fencing Club) of Livorno, on Italy's west coast, invited me to a gala. I went with Alessandro Puccini and his coach, Antonio DiCiolo. I stayed almost two weeks, training in the club every night and enjoying the Italian food, but getting in trouble with my old elbow and ankle injuries and a daily nosebleed. In addition, for some reason I couldn't sleep for more than three hours a night.

One of my sparring partners at the Fides Club was young Salvatore Sanzo, who would become World Champion in 2001. I also bought a car in Livorno. Back in Kiev, I owned a miracle of the Ukrainian auto industry. It needed repairs almost every week. In Livorno, I bought…a miracle of the Russian auto industry, a Lada.

Early one Friday morning, I and my new miracle set out for the long drive to Budapest, the scene of the next World Cup. The quickest route lay through Austria, but since I still didn't have a visa, I had to drive through Slovenia. They held me for seven hours at the Slovenian border because of some bureaucratic mix-up.

It was nearly midnight when I reached Budapest. I couldn't find the Ukrainian team. I called my friend Mark Marsi, who told me that he owned a place where I could spend the night. Mark and I drove there, he gave me the key, and I drove him home. Then I headed back toward the apartment. It was almost 24 hours since I had set out. I was fantasizing about a good hot shower and a nice, long sleep. But when I got to the building, I couldn't get in. Mark had given me his apartment key, but not the building key.

It was late March and the nights were still quite cold, but I had no choice but to sleep in the car. I ran the engine for a while to get the car warm so that I could sleep. Before turning it off, I looked at my watch: it was three o'clock in the morning. I slept until 6, when the cold woke me again.

I ran the engine until the car warmed up and slept again until 9, when I drove to the fencing venue, where I found my team and the address of our hotel.

With this preparation, I won the World Cup the next day.

We have a saying that goes something like this: "Without the right paper, you're nothing; with the right paper, you're the boss."

I returned to Ukraine to prepare for the next event, the UAP World Cup in Paris. As usual, I needed to get a visa to travel to France, and as was often the case, I had to do it on my own. It just so happened that I decided to get mine on May 11, 1995, the day that President Bill Clinton was visiting Kiev for the first time. I spent the morning trying to get them, and was told that the papers would be ready after the lunch break.

Liudmila and little Elena were with me. No sense in keeping them waiting. I decided to take them home and return to pick up the visa. It would mean leaving most of my identification at the Embassy, but so what?

I was on the highway with only one more turn to get home when a cop stopped me.

"You can't turn here," he said.

"My daughter is very tired and needs to get home," I said, showing him my SBU identification, showing that I was a member of the State Security Agency.

It didn't impress him. "Keep driving," he said.

No big deal, I thought. I could just drive another kilometer and make the turn there. But there was a cop at that intersection too.

"You can't turn here," he said.

The day was hot, we were all tired, and I still had to get to the French Embassy to get my visa. I decided to turn back before we reached the highway from the airport. But the cops were stopping all traffic moving toward the city.

I waved to an officer. "When will Clinton come by?"

"Fifteen minutes," he said.

I thought about my options. There's no solid divider on that stretch of highway, just a strip of grass. I decided to drive toward the airport, then, out of sight of the police, make a U-turn across the grass divider and head back. It was stupid and, in principle, dangerous, but I was at the boiling point.

My car was the only one on the highway. I drove for a while and wanted to make my U-turn, but just at that moment, I noticed a cop with a Kalashnikov. So I drove on, and then I saw the beginning of President Clinton's escort. I stopped my car on the grass divider (as I said, I was the only car on the road). We got out of the car and watched Clinton drive by.

Then a flood of cars came surging by; they'd been held up for hours. Would I get a chance for that U-turn now?

Just at the moment I had decided to turn, two police cars, sirens blaring, blocked me. An officer jumped out with eyes like two silver dollars.

"Papers!" he shouted.

I showed him my SBU identification. His tone changed, but he still wanted to see my driver's license.

"I don't have it on me," I told him.

He drew his gun.

"Do you know who was driving past this place?" he shouted.

"I don't care," I told him. "I was just trying to get my little girl home and then go back to the French Embassy for my papers."

The cop turned to his partner. They unscrewed my license plates and kept them. That meant that I would have to go to Police Headquarters to get them back. Usually this meant a two-year suspension of the license.

But remember that saying: "With the right piece of paper, you're the boss!" I was a lieutenant of the SBU and a world-class athlete. I made the necessary phone calls before going to Paris. After I returned, when I went to headquarters, the chief of police himself gave me my plates back.

I promised not to do anything like that again; he wished me good luck with my fencing.

Papers in hand, I finally got to Kiev's Borispol Airport on my way to the World Cup. I checked in, got past passport control, and went to the bar for a cup of coffee. There I saw a girl whose face I recognized: Natasha Medvedeva, the best Ukrainian tennis player and one of the top 25 in the world. I had seen her on TV from time to time.

"May I drink my coffee in your company?" I asked her.

She nodded, and I introduced myself to her. It was the beginning of a friendship that continues to this day.

Oh, yes. I took ninth place in Paris, but with everything that was going on, I have no recollection of the tournament!

All this time, my daughter was growing, becoming a beautiful little girl. At the age of eighteen months she knew the Russian alphabet and even a fair number of English words. She was in constant motion, never giving anyone a moment's rest. Any time I was in Kiev, between tournaments and camps, I loved to play with her and teach her.

The last training camp before the World Championships in July was on the Black Sea. I was in good shape and looking forward to the competition. The third session one day was volleyball. Someone on the other team went up for a kill and I went up to block him. I made the block because I jumped higher, but the result was that I came down later, on his foot. A sharp pain, like an electric shock, went through my right ankle, and I figured immediately that I could forget about the World Championships. In moments, my ankle looked like it belonged to a sumo wrestler. I have had ankle injuries throughout my career, but this one was the worst. Normally, I'd recover in 7 – 10 days, but there was no time. I was ready to stay home.

We were training at the Olympic Center with many other sports teams. Somehow one of the coaches found a masseuse from a volleyball team.

When she showed up, I thought that it was all for nothing: there was no way she could make me ready in time for the championships.

But never say never! A miracle took place.

Several times each day, she gave me a great massage, so that my muscles would stay strong even if I didn't train. She would "ice massage" my sprained ankle for twenty minutes; then, while it was still numb, she would force me to move it, to move my toes. When it started hurting, she'd go back to the ice massage. Exercise, ice, exercise, ice…

After two days, after an ice massage, she made me swim in the Black Sea. I wouldn't have believed it possible, but I did it. On the third day, I was running—slowly—in the stadium.

In addition, one of the fencing trainers, Alexandr Obolensky, was doing a kind of magic massage every day. He would move his hands around my ankle *without touching it*. It seemed to work!

The day of the injury, I had been pessimistic. By the second day, I started to believe that everything would work out. These two wonderful people and my native confidence would help me recover.

I fenced in the World Championships after all. They were held at The Hague, the administrative capital of the Netherlands (Amsterdam is the constitutional capital. Don't ask!) . My ankle was heavily taped, and I was limited to making only proper footwork.

I made it to the last four.

In the first bout of the semis, to everyone's astonishment, José do Guerra of Spain beat Elvis Gregory of Cuba 15 – 14. I was matched with Dmitri Shevchenko, and both of us were sure that the winner of our bout would be the next World Champion. Dima ate me alive, 15 – 5. I shared the bronze medal with Elvis Gregory.

I won the overall World Cup for the fourth year in a row. No fencer had ever done that before. And just this once, after my injury, I was satisfied with the bronze medal.

After the championships, we had a party. After a few drinks, I got a strong desire to try some marijuana. After all, I was in Holland, where it's legal. Finally I found some.

At first, I didn't feel anything. A few minutes later, I noticed that the glass in the window was changing its shape. Suddenly, I couldn't tell if my heart was beating. I got scared. I started to move crazily. My body was out of control. I found a teammate and asked for help. After a glass of water, I felt a little better.

That was an experiment I never tried again, and I advice you to do the same. You're an athlete. You need to keep your mind and body in top shape, like a finely-tuned instrument. What's the point of putting yourself at risk?

Fencing at the World University Games in Fukuoka, Japan, wouldn't start until the 26th of August. I accepted an invitation for a training camp and some relaxation in Croatia. We would be staying on the beautiful, historic island of Hvar, in the Adriatic Sea. I was traveling with Liudmila and Elena and some friends in a party of three cars. The plan was to drive to Zagreb, the capital of Croatia, catch a bus to Split, on the coast, then take a two-hour ferryboat ride to Hvar.

We arrived in Zagreb in good order, but after we checked into our hotel, and were ready to turn in for the night Sanjin Kovacic, one of the camp's organizers, came in, obviously upset. He had impossible news: *a war broke out today!*

Actually, there had been sporadic fighting ever since Croatia declared its independence from Yugoslavia in 1991. But starting in May, 1995, the Croatians had begun to retake land that the Serbs had won from them. Sanjin was bringing news of the start of the final Croatian offensives.

He tried to reassure us: "You're all safe here," he said. "The Serbian missiles won't hit us."

Wow! Thanks!

(We would have been even more ecstatic if we'd known that Serbian missiles had actually *hit* Zagreb that May!)

I don't know how everybody else was feeling, but I was worried, not just for myself, but for my family.

Sanjin was supposed to go to Hvar with us, but he was mobilized into the armed forces and had to stay in Zagreb, awaiting orders.

The next day, we took the bus from Zagreb to Split. It was sad to see the beautiful countryside in ruins: bridges destroyed, bullet holes scarring the facades of buildings, deserted houses and towns.

In the end, we reached Hvar without any trouble. A few days later, we heard that Croatia had won the war. The nation celebrated.

Several days later, we were eating dinner at a restaurant. We were having a good time and left Elena free to walk around. We were in a good position to watch all the exits: she couldn't get out of the dining room. Outside was a terrace with a view of the sea. Below it, six meters down, was a swimming pool surrounded by a marble patio. The terrace ended in a wall that was higher than Elena's head. So we were relaxing and enjoying our meal.

Suddenly our friend, the coach Alexandr Tikhomirov jumped out of his chair, kicked off his sandals, and ran toward the terrace. When I looked past him, I could see that Elena was standing on top of the terrace wall, oblivious to the 6-metre drop and the swimming pool below. She balanced there for a moment…it was too late for me to do anything…and Aleksandr caught her. She thought it was just a game that Aleksandr was playing with her. I thought differently!

Later he told me he figured that if she had heard him coming, she might have become frightened and fallen. That was why he had kicked off his sandals.

After this vacation, which had been much less relaxing than anticipated, we drove back to Kiev, where I trained briefly before the University Games.

It had been a long, stressful year, and I was tired and unmotivated for this final event. I felt more like a tourist than an athlete, trying to have a good time in Japan.

In the Games, I met Elvis Gregory of Cuba in the quarterfinals. The Cubans had sent only Elvis and a sabre fencer to Fukuoka, and Elvis was hugely motivated—to show that he could win without a coach or the support of his teammates.

The bout started out well for me. I scored the first five touches, making each of them in a different way. Elvis was being blown away. So he faked an injury. I could see that he wasn't hurt; he just needed to take a break to figure out what to do with me. Sixty seconds after the break, he had tied the score 5 – 5! Either of us could have won it, but Elvis' motivation paid off and he beat me, as I recall, 15 – 14. Then he beat Shevchenko for the championship.

In the foil team event I didn't fence well at all. I wasn't even inspired by my teammates, who were fencing well and doing their best.

But I did leave Fukuoka with a medal. Just like two years before, I was a reserve on the epee team. I wasn't even with them when they fenced—I was back in the athletes' village. But they fenced really well, finishing second to a strong Hungarian team. I arrived just in time for the medal ceremony. I got a silver medal, which I gave to the trainer in charge of the epee squad.

1995—1996

I wanted to win the European Championship. I was coming off a good win in Berlin and I wanted to win a title, to be recognized as the best in Europe on that day. Besides my overall World Cups, the only *title* I held was the championship at the '93 University Games in Buffalo. You could almost say that I had reached a point in my career where I was tired of winning the overall World Cup if it meant that I wasn't going to win a title.

> I was tired of winning overall World Cup titles without every winning the World Championship.

The overall World Cup has a different psychology. You can't go into a season planning to win it. You have to pile up placements in World Cup events, bit by bit, step by step, touch by touch. No one event counts more than another. Toward the end of the season, you can start to think about your overall standing.

It's much more difficult to win a title event like the European Championships, the World Championships, or the Olympics. You have to be the best on exactly that day. There's more pressure on the top fencers and more of a chance of a fluke or surprise victory from a lower-ranked fencer. That's why these victories have a higher value.

You can win or lose by a fluke. But you always know when you are ready to win. You feel that your time has arrived.

That's how I felt going into the European Championships. I was almost 26 years old: a time of maturity for a competitive fencer.

The tournament was held at Keszthely, a lovely, old-fashioned resort town on the shores of Lake Balaton in Hungary.

I had no trouble before meeting Shevchenko in the semis. Just as at The Hague a few months earlier, we both knew that this would be the gold medal bout. This time it was my day; I won a very difficult bout.

The final event at Keszthely consisted of the final bouts from all the disciplines. I was up against the young and promising Italian, Taddei. But I was the heavy favorite. If there had been betting, the odds would have been 25 – 1 in my favor. But still, I was really nervous. (Check back through this book to see how often I was nervous before a final: not often.)

The men's foil title bout was the last of all. The great European epee champion, Arnd Schmitt, had just finished his bout, taking the European title. Somehow, he felt my nervousness. He put his arm around my shoulder.

> "Don't think too much about the title. Just fence the way you fenced all those World Cups."

"Don't think too much about the title," he said. "Just fence the way you fenced all those World Cups. Just be yourself."

And you know, it helped!

I didn't give my opponent one second to question my superiority. It was fast and painless, 15 – 4. It felt good, really good, to know that I held the title of the best fencer on the continent of Europe.

The World Cup season, as always, began with the tournaments in Vienna and St. Petersburg, where I finished third and second respectively, losing both times to Shevchenko. The second defeat was especially memorable. I led 13 – 8 and was blown away, 15 – 13.

How does a bout have such wild swings? When both fencers are at the same level, chaos sometimes rules. Our sport depends so much on subtle feeling—for distance, rhythm, and so on—that a momentary lapse can lead to a dramatic slide. An opponent can turn the tables on you very quickly, and it's difficult to turn them to your side once that happens.

Next came Havana. I was Chief of the Ukrainian delegation here, which was both an honor and a responsibility. I arrived with four young women epeeists who were also there for the World Cup. I got to the fencing hall before their competition to check things out. They told me that we had had a visitor from the Ukrainian Embassy to Havana. He had asked whether we had brought vodka and caviar for resale, and when the girls said no, he had turned around and left.

It's nice to see such support from your countrymen!

In the men's foil, I was bout to fence Ingo Weissenborn of Germany, the 1991 World Champion, to reach the final eight. During the pause before this round, I went to check on my epeeists. A few minutes later, my former teammate Slava Grigoriev ran up to me. He was fencing for Kazakhstan at that time; now he lives in the USA.

"Get going!"

"But…"

"Now! You've been called. You already have a red card (penalty touch)!"

In a few moments I was standing on the strip ready to fence, but Ingo wasn't there. Some Italian fencers, grinning, said that the referee had showed a black card. I was disqualified.

> They told me that I had received a black card for reporting late to the strip. I was disqualified!

This was serious. I hadn't come all this way to get a black card. Besides, if I was disqualified, the Ukrainian Federation would make me pay for all of my expenses.

I went straight to the top. I talked to René Roch, the President of the FIE and Jeno Kamuti, the President of the European Federation. They understood my problem, but they also knew what the rules were.

"Talk to Ingo," they told me. "The bout can go on only

if he agrees to it."

Thank you, Ingo!

His decision to fence the bout meant a lot to me.

I beat him (sorry, Ingo!) and had to face Taddei to make the semis. I broke my last foil against him. Maged Shaker lent me his, but I couldn't hit anything with it. I lost 15 – 14 to finish fifth.

In the end, I won only one World Cup that season. At the last event of the season, I took a disastrous 33rd place, losing my *first bout* to Ralf Bissdorf of Germany.

Yes, Bissdorf would go on to be a very strong fencer. But clearly, something was going on with me...and my head...

The Olympics: Atlanta 1996

As the only Ukrainian foil fencer to qualify for the Olympics so far, I was on my own as far as finding a place for training and sparring. My dad and I went to Poland to train with their Olympic team in a series of three camps. Each camp would be 7 – 10 days long with a break of two or three days between camps.

The first camp was at Zielona Gora, a university town up in the mountains that had an Olympic training center. The chief of the Polish men's foil team, Stanislaw Szymanski, led the program. We would walk in the hills, do a lot of general athletics, play basketball and soccer, do a lot of footwork drills. That was it—general preparation.

The next camp was at Wladyslawowo, a very small town on the seacoast of

> The first camp stressed general physical preparation. The second was balanced between general conditioning, fencing, and footwork. The third stressed sparring and individual lessons—a typical final camp for a specific event.

Pomerania, near the German border, also with a training center. This time, the balance shifted more toward fencing and footwork, but there was still a lot of general athletics and games. Here I started individual lessons with my father.

The third camp was in nearby Cetniewo. Here the focus was on sparring, footwork, and lessons. It was a typical final camp to prepare for a specific competition—in this case, the Olympic Games.

"D-Day" would be July 22, 1996.

Another of my father's students, Alexei Bryzgalov, was also hoping to go to the Olympics. He had taken third place at the zone qualifiers in May. Unfortunately, only the top two qualifiers from the zone would go. Only a miracle would get Alexei to Atlanta, and the miracle took place. The Belgian Federation wouldn't let one of its qualifiers take part for some reason, so Alexei got the "lucky ticket."

I was in great shape heading into the Olympics. Alexei used to complain that he could hardly touch me at all.

The Ukrainian delegation was the first to arrive at the Olympic Village in Sydney. Looking back on the bustling Village in Barcelona '92, it was strange to find the place empty. We had a great time with short lines everywhere, especially for a new laser game called "Q-sar." As the Village filled up, though, the lines grew longer and the feeling that the Village was our own private playground was gone.

But there were compensations. Sometimes we would get a sighting of some celebrity. One day I saw a dense crowd of people, and when I checked, Muhammad Ali was at the center, chatting with people and letting them take his picture. I also got a glimpse of Dolph Lundgren, the action movie star. He was actually the leader of the US Modern Pentathlon Team. It was a case of life imitating art, since Dolph had starred in a move called "Pentathlon" a few years earlier. Despite his ambitions as a serious actor, his most famous role probably remains one of his first: that of Ivan Drago, the villainous Russian boxer in *Rocky IV*.

Dolph Lundgren had a friend on the Olympic pentath-lon team from Georgia (the independent country, not the US State). He went to the building where the Georgians were staying, knocked on the door, and asked for his friend. Whoever it was that answered the door went back into the room and said, "Drago's outside looking for you!"

In retrospect, the early arrival wasn't good for me. There wasn't much to do in the Village, and I only went to the Olympic City a few times (an hour after my last visit, a bomb went off, and I didn't go back). I lost a little of my sharpness and the trip from the Village to the training site was horrendous: it was a 90-minute round trip by bus. Once, a driver drove us for an hour and a half to the wrong site, then another hour and a half to correct his error. All of the monotony, I think, killed the competitive edge I had brought with me from the training camps, and I probably had lost the peak of my conditioning a few days before I was supposed to fence.

In addition, I had a dilemma in my personal life which was eating me up. It preyed on my mind throughout the games, leaving me restless and nervous.

My first bout was against the South Korean Yong-Kook Kim. I raced out to a 7 – 1 lead, but started to hurt physi-cally. The bout may have looked easy—I won 15 – 4—but it cost me. Waiting for me next was my old buddy, Ye Chong of China, always a difficult opponent. He had beaten Alex Koch in a very close match, 15 – 13. It was a slow, careful, tactical bout. I took an early 5 – 1 lead, but Chong equal-ized, taking advantage of mistakes in my attacks. I went out in front, 6 – 5, but just before time ran out, he tied the score again, 6 – 6. The coin toss gave Chong the priority. One minute of sudden death remained to fence…and if there was no touch, Chong would have the victory. I attacked; Chong counterattacked. If I hit, I had the right of way. I felt his attack hit; I didn't know if mine had arrived. I looked at the lights and saw that mine was on. I'd won, 7 – 6.

Then I made the same mistake I made in Barcelona when I beat Elvis Gregory to get to the gold medal bout: I broke down and cried. The tension had been so great that I couldn't control myself. With the tears, I drained myself mentally and emotionally, losing alertness and focus. My tank was now half-empty.

Next was Lionel Plumenail. He had beaten me on occasion and started out strongly. Throughout the bout, I was two or three touches behind. Using all my willpower, I evened the score at 10 – 10. I even made it 11 – 10. But now my tank was absolutely empty. I felt dizzy and started to see double. I asked the referee for a short break, but he wouldn't allow it. Within seconds, Plumenail had a 14 – 11 lead. I fought back to 14 – 13. We made simultaneous attacks. He hit; I missed. I had lost not only the bout, but my dream of winning the Olympics. I wound up in sixth place.

Starting Over

1996—1997

After the Olympics, I had reached a crossroads, not only for myself but for my family. I had fallen hard for a woman who wasn't my wife, a Dutch girl I had met on the road. I had to resolve this triangle as soon as the Olympics were over.

Right after I got back from Atlanta, I told Liudmila that I had decided to leave her and start a new life away from Ukraine. She was bitter, and I could understand her suffering. And my heart ached for my little daughter Elena, now almost three years old, whom I felt I was losing forever.

I was going to post-Olympic receptions given by the President of Ukraine, the Mayor of Kiev, and so on. During these events, I would often find myself sitting alone, almost crying. My heart was with my daughter and my parents, but my mind was far away.

Shortly afterward, I had to go into the hospital for minor surgery, the removal of a cyst. During the recovery, I had a lot of time to think about my life and future.

Still recovering, I went with my mother to Lake Balaton in Hungary. It was autumn already. The fencing season was beginning. I had to get my head together after this period of turmoil. At Lake Balaton, I started to prepare for the season. Fencing was still my life, and I threw myself into it.

The first tournament of the season was in Berlin. I drove to Holland to visit my girlfriend and train there. Then on to Berlin for a tough competition that would be a good check on my preparation so far. I lost to Alex Koch for the gold medal and won 1000 DM for second place. I almost lost that money to a problem at the German-Polish border, but the problem was resolved when I showed the guards my trophy cup and my picture from the tournament.

The World Cup in Vienna opened the new Olympic cycle. After my private turmoil, I could focus on fencing almost exclusively. In Vienna, I beat the '96 Olympic bronze medalist, Franck Boidin of France, to win first place. The score was 15 – 6.

Next stop, St. Petersburg. I was on cruise control until the finals: 15 – 6, 15 – 7, 15 – 8, 15 – 6, 15 – 8. In the bout for first place, I met Wolfgang Wienand of Germany, who had taken fourth place at the Olympics. He was fencing his best against me, and the score mounted to 14 – 14.

The referee called, *"Allez!"* I attacked. Wolfgang ducked and my point found nothing but air. Another second place.

Two weeks later, I threw my clothing and fencing gear into my car, jumped in, and drove to the Netherlands to start a life as a foreigner, far away from my family, friends, and country. The fact that it was my choice somehow didn't make it any easier. I met the New Year in a new land, starting a new life.

Fencing alone wouldn't be enough to survive now, the way it always had before. I needed to find a job and start earning money. Here I found good luck in the person of Maarten Jansen, the president of the OKK Fencing Club in The Hague. The club had its own building and I could train myself while giving fenc-

I found good luck in the person of Maarten Jansen, president of the OKK Fencing Club in The Hague.

ing lessons. Here I got my first student, Tashunka Jansen, Maarten's son. In time, the Jansen family would become my family.

> Day by day, I added new mateial to my lessons. I began to sense new possibilities in timing, distance, and bladework. My coaching became an experimental laboratory.
>
> I tried to combine the logic of the Russian school with the creativity of the Ukrainian.

It's fair to say that as of 1997, I knew a great deal about actually fencing, but in the realm of coaching I had a lot to learn. It wasn't difficult because I had been lucky enough to work with many fine coaches, starting with my father. At the beginning, I used to start by giving my father's lessons, putting in bits and pieces from other coaches. But day by day, I started adding my own stuff. I began to sense new possibilities in timing, distance, and bladework. In a way, my coaching became an experimental laboratory for my fencing. I gave my students new actions that had worked for me. And, perhaps most importantly, I tried to integrate the logical, disciplined bladework of the classical Russian school with the intuitive, creative actions of the Ukrainian school.

In January, I skipped the Havana and Zurich World Cups and went only to Paris, where I lost to Elvis Gregory and took third place. I was really glad to see my friends from the Russian team. I had hardly spoken Russian in almost a month. I was homesick.

Meanwhile, I was negotiating with Merten Mauritz about a coaching job in Vienna. We made a deal and I was to leave for Vienna at the beginning of February.

My last evening in Rotterdam, I decided to go to the casino and try my luck at blackjack. I parked my car next to the central railroad station and went to play.

No, I didn't break the bank—either the casino's or mine. I broke even and had a good time. When I returned to my car, the glass on the passenger's side looked wet, although it hadn't been raining. On a closer look, someone had tried to break in. The glass was crazed with cracks. I had to spend a few more days in Holland getting it fixed. Then I packed everything into my car and drove to Vienna.

By this time, I was beginning to feel like a vagabond, moving from place to place with nowhere to call home. I took an apartment near the center of Vienna. My job called on me to coach three days a week from 4:00 to 9:00 p.m. The rest of my time was my own, for training or leisure.

My first problem as a coach in Vienna was that I wasn't dealing with serious fencers. My students were fencing for fun. I just couldn't get my mind around it. I had come up in the Soviet system, where "fun" was not an objective, and I had become a professional athlete. I had always been goal-oriented, trying to achieve something. I had paid for being among the best in the world through injuries, long training sessions, "blood, toil, tears, and sweat."

> It was hard to adapt to fencers who weren't serious. I couldn't get my mind around the idea of fencing "just for fun." I was from the Soviet system. I still think it's important to set goals.

I think that a lot of coaches from the former Soviet Union have had to make this adjustment. Now that I'm a "Westerner," I can understand the concept of fencing for enjoyment. Still, I think that even if you are fencing for fun, you need to set goals for yourself. That gives you a challenge and the satisfaction of achievement. I can deal with fencers who have goals.

> People were start-
> ing to say that I was
> washed up. And I was
> almost beginning to
> believe them.

But starting out in Vienna, it was driving me crazy. My students would claim that they wanted great results, their mouths would form the words, "I'm willing to train"…and then, before an important tournament, they'd disappear into the mountains for a ski vacation. Was this the Western mentality?

At the beginning of March I came down with the flu. I had to forget about fencing in Venice. I lost a lot of points in the world rankings that year, because I didn't defend my third places in Zurich and Venice and my fifth place in Havana.

A month later, after fencing in Paris, I went to Bordeaux for a special tournament. It's a great event, attended by many strong fencers. I won it this time, taking a hollow revenge on Plumenail, 15 – 8, for my Olympic defeat, but coming away some splendid loot: 18 Napoleon gold coins, plus four cases, and one 12-liter bottle (a bottle with the wonderful name of Balthazar) of fine Bordeaux wine.

The rest of the season seemed more or less awful. Instead of taking lessons, I had to give them. Instead of touching, I had to let my students touch me. I wasn't ready for that yet.
And I missed my family.

Already a lot of coaches, trainers, and fencing experts had started to say it:

> *Golubitsky is finished. He had a good run,*
> *but his best days are clearly behind him. He'll*
> *never have a top result again.*

I was beginning to think the same, to tell the truth. I didn't see how I was going to beat the world's top fencers without top lessons and proper sparring. My results sagged. I took two ninth places and a seventeenth. Just at the end of the season, I was invited to fence in a new tournament, a world cup candidates' tournament, in Porto, Portugal. I lost to Wienand, 15 – 11. It wasn't a great bout, but the medal I won showed me a light at the end of the tunnel.

At the end of April, I once again threw everything I owned into my car and headed for Holland. I wanted to be with my girlfriend, even though it wasn't a good decision from a fencing point of view. But I had a chance for a job in Holland and once again dove into uncertainty.

Breakthrough in Cape Town

The time of the World Championships approached. Once again, I had the opportunity to train in Poland, so I could get in some decent training. This time, the Ukrainian team was there, too, so that I could train with my father.

The camp started out in a very frustrating way. I was acting as if it was the year, or the years, before. In my head, I was just as strong, but my body was playing tricks on me. Sometimes my attacks were too fast; I would pick the wrong moment and miss. But my father found ways to calm me down, keep me going, and get me into the best shape possible under the circumstances. The camp lasted for fourteen days, and then I drove to Kiev, thoroughly fed up with myself.

Back in Kiev, I gave some interviews to the sports reporters. I told them very frankly that I wasn't going to the World Championships to win a medal, but just to see how well I could still fence. There were a number of fencers who were at the top of their games this year and that I had no desire to fence: Shevchenko, Chong, Plumenail, and Gregory.

I wasn't frightened of them in any way, I explained; I would simply rather not meet them on the fencing strip.

Finally we flew down to Cape Town. My father didn't come with me, perhaps out of a superstitious desire to help me! He hadn't been with me when I won the World University Games or the European Championships. Maybe he thought the best he could do for me was to stay home.l

I fell in love with Cape Town immediately: great climate, wonderful scenery, delicious food, and great wines.

But all this beauty contrasted with the social situation in a country where the traces of apartheid were still all too evident. (The first multi-racial elections had been held only in 1994.) We were advised not to walk alone outdoors, to stay in groups, to keep to our hotel after dark. Fencers from several countries complained that money had been stolen from their hotel rooms during the Veterans World Championships. A French veteran fencer had not only been robbed at knifepoint; he had been cut as well.

There were private security guards everywhere. Many shops had stickers on the windows: *These premises are protected by armed security."*

During the competition, we were having an ongoing card game among the fencers, with players wandering freely between rooms. Hotel security put an end to that: a guard came in and told us to keep our doors locked.

These annoyances took some of the luster from what was still a wonderful city.

I was seeded seventh, my lowest world ranking of the last five years. It was no surprise, considering the turmoil of my life and all the pressures that had cut into my training time. I needed to prove something: that I wasn't finished as a fencer, and that I could still fence at a top level. I wanted to prove myself with every single touch.

On the evening of July 15th, 1997, I got the printout of next day's tableau of 64 for the World Championships. I wasn't delighted. My draw included Chong, Shevchenko, and Plumenail, assuming that we all held form—three of the four fencers I had told reporters I didn't want to face. I couldn't complain, though—I could have drawn Gregory as well!

On top of all that, my first-round bout was against the Dane, Nicolas Guilbert, who had made me sweat several times in the past…

He would do so this time, too.

The first bout of a competition is very important for me. It tells me how ready I am, both physically and mentally. It gives me a sign: is this my day—or not? It's like when an orchestra tunes up: you're checking the strings of your violin, making little adjustments in order to produce great music.

> The first bout of a competition is very important. It tells me how ready I am, both physically and mentally. It's like tuning up: you make little adjustments.

After the first two three-minute periods against Guilbert, all the signs were pointing…straight down. I was attacking too much and too fast. He led 12 – 10, hitting me again and again by closing the distance on me.

I had one minute to get my head together, to replay my errors, notice them, and erase them. Once I've done this, I have no right to be hit the same way again. I won't allow it! Now he's lost his advantage. He thinks he's fencing against the "me" he was facing a minute ago. But I know different.

One minute late, I had scored five touches and was shaking his hand.

Next, as expected, was the first fencer from my blacklist: my Chinese rival, Ye Chong, perhaps the best Chinese foil fencer ever. I had already fenced him many times, mostly holding an advantage; but even each victory had its special torments. I told myself that I had to take control of the bout from the start if I wanted to win; otherwise it would be a lottery.

The previous bout had given me the sense of attack, and I used it, rushing out to a five touch lead that I held almost to the end and winning 15 – 11.

One touch at a time. One bout at a time.

The seedings were holding up. To reach the last eight, I would have to cross foils with Dmitri Shevchenko, the second fencer from my blacklist. He had beaten me many times over the years and was always a tough opponent, not just because of his great talent and experience, but also because of the sheer *reach* this 6'5" lefthander had at his disposal. We knew each other very well and there was going to be very little opportunity to come up with a surprise.

From my former USSR teammates, I had heard about one "dirty trick" that Shevchenko liked to use. Every so often, while retreating, he would add to his prodigious reach by throwing his foil forward into his opponent's attack like a javelin. He had a chance of hitting this way, while his opponent had no chance to reach him. Of course it was illegal—there's a specific rule against it in the book—but it was hard to detect from the side, because it would look as if he had dropped his foil because of his opponent's beat or parry. If Shevchenko missed, the referee would just stop the action, while if he hit, he would score the touch.

Before the bout, I asked the referee, the American Greg Massialas, to watch out for this. He promised he'd keep an eye out.

The spectators really got into this bout, an all-out war between two former Soviet teammates. The Russians were cheering for Dmitri; the Ukrainians were yelling for me. At the start, I was constantly on the defensive. Dmitri was all over me: I was down 6 – 2, then 7 – 3. I went on the offensive and evened the score at 7 – 7.

With the score tied, I prepared another attack, moving into his half of the strip, but staying out of reach. I stepped forward, he took a step back...and the light went on—against me! *Dmitri had thrown his foil.*

The referee signaled the touch. I tore my mask off, telling Greg that it was the "javelin" action. It's hard to get a referee to change a decision once he's awarded the touch. Greg stood for a moment, thinking, replaying the action in his mind. Finally, he made the right call. He annulled the touch and showed Shevchenko a yellow card. The score was still tied.

The Russian coaches and spectators crowded around the referee, shouting their protests. The atmosphere grew heated. I was trying not to get caught up in the excitement; I simply kept telling myself: "Keep the pressure on! Move forward!"

On the command to fence, I pressed forward...and unbelievably, Dmitri did the same thing again! I didn't have to be dramatic this time; all I had to do was look at Massialas, who showed Dmitri a red card—penalty touch!

On the next touch, Dmitri grabbed my blade with his unarmed hand—another penalty touch! Dmitri had momentarily fallen apart, and the tide of battle had turned decisively in my favor. I won 15 – 11.

To reach the final four and reserve a place on the podium, I had to fence Benny Wendt of Austria. I went all out and won going away, 15 – 7.

There was an hour break before the final four. I rested up for my semifinal bout against Lionel Plumenail. He'd kept me off the podium in Atlanta. He was another member of my "do not want to fence this guy" list. But somehow, the list had lost its terror.

I was all over him in the beginning, mostly on the attack, and went out to a 7 – 3 lead. Then I lost focus, but still went the first break with a narrow lead, 8 – 7. During the break I refocused, and in the second period I imposed my will, outscoring him 7 – 2 to reach the final, where Young Ho Kim of South Korea was waiting for me, having defeated Haibin Wang of China, 15 – 14.

I was on the threshold of the goal I had sought for years. I was focused. I wasn't nervous. I wasn't thinking about "what-ifs." I was ready. But so was Kim.

It would become one of the most dramatic bouts in my career, but it didn't start out that way. I was leading, as I said, 11 – 3, using every technique in my arsenal, and people were saying that it was a mismatch, Golubitsky is simply too strong for the poor Korean, and that's it's no fun to watch a final where one fencer is so hopelessly outclassed.

My parents were back in Kiev. The bout was on TV, but my parents' apartment couldn't get the channel. Liudmila, though, was able to get the live broadcast, and she called my parents periodically to give them updates on the bout. When the score reached 11 – 3 in my favor, she told them that she would call again when I had won.

At 11 – 3, I wasn't exactly feeling overconfident, but I did lose a little concentration. Meanwhile, as Kim's trainer later told me, Kim had been fencing with too much respect for me. At 11 – 3, he had nothing to lose, he was tired of fencing scared, and he started to fence up to his ability. He made a series of well-timed countertempos; then his instinct kicked in and he developed an uncanny sense of when to make a simple attack and when to make a compound attack. In a 13-second burst, he scored six touches to make it 11 – 9, and a few moments later, the score was tied at 11.

Back in Kiev, my father and mother were left sitting, waiting for the phone to ring. Any second now… Any minute now… But the minutes stretched on endlessly, and the phone didn't ring…

I remember clearly that I didn't panic. But at the same time, I didn't know how to stop him. The score went to 14 – 14. One touch against me, and my dream would go up in smoke. I decided to go on the defensive. The next moment, Kim put everything he had on an incredibly deep attack. I felt the tip of his foil against my skin…

Finally, Dad asked my mother to call Liudmila. He watched helplessly as Mom listened.

I took a last-second parry, losing control of my foil.

Kim threw up his arms in triumph.

But the scoring machine remained silent!

My legs were weary; I could hardly raise my arms, and my fingers were stiff.

Still on the defensive, I continued to fight.

Kim came forward, intending another long attack.

I'd been counterattacking consistently. This time, I showed him a false counterattack, and he bit on it, lunging too early and too short.

That was what I was looking for! I took circle-6 and riposted with a lunge…

> I'd been making a lot of counterattacks. This time I showed him a false counterattack, and he lunged.

Mom hung up the phone and turned to my father. "Sergei won. 15 – 14," she told him.

Back in Cape Town, I had collapsed on the strip, crying like a baby.

My dream was a reality. Now I was standing on the podium, smiling broadly, listening to the national anthem of my Ukraine.

I was the Champion of the World.

On my return to Kiev, my father and I watched the bout on videotape. When it was over, he couldn't hide his tears.

The season still wasn't over; the World University Games remained. These, my fourth and last University Games, would be held in Sicily. Seeded first, I faced Rolando Tucker of Cuba for the gold medal. Behind throughout the bout, Rolando caught up and tied the score at 13. I tried to provoke his attack and hit him with parry-ripostes, but Rolando succeeded in finding his way past my parries and pulled out the bout, 15 – 13. I wasn't too upset: I was still savoring the feeling of being World Champion. I didn't need to "take revenge" on anyone or think about what might have been.

Besides that, Ukraine did great at this Universiade. We led the combined medal standings in all sports throughout most of the Games. Only on the last day did a push by the US drop us into second. And in fencing, Ukraine took first overall, winning four gold medals, one silver, and two bronzes. We came ahead of Hungary, Italy, Russia, and Cuba.

Best of all, my father, as chief of the foil team, earned a personal triumph as well.

There was one day of rest between the individual and team foil events. All the other teams were taking a break, relaxing before the final day of the endless fencing year.

But not our young Ukraine squad, which consisted of Alexei Bryzgalov, Alexei Krugliak, Oleg Matseichuk, and me. On paper, we might have been overmatched, but our spirit was high.

My father led a short outdoor training session. We ran for a bit; we did some footwork and stretched. The idea was to get rid of the accumulated lactic acid in our muscles and build team spirit for the day ahead.

Dad asked me for my opinion about when we had enough. He couldn't feel exactly how tired we were, but I sure could. I reminded him of a saying he had taught me:

"Better to train a little too little than a little too much."

We ended the session in a good mood.

By that time in my career, I had already developed my own personal routine for the day of the tournament. Every experienced fencer has one. Assuming I was already at the competition city, I used to wake up three hours before the start of the competition. If it began at 8:30 in the morning, I would be sure to wake up at 5:30 in order to be ready and alert for the first bout. Sometimes I'd hit the shower or watch some TV before breakfast.

That early in the morning, especially with your pre-competition nerves, it's no secret that you don't want to eat anything—your body is still asleep!

Nevertheless, *breakfast is an important part of tournament preparation*. During your first warm-up, you start burning calories. If you haven't nourished yourself in the morning, you have to start drawing your energy from your body's reserves. By the end of the tournament you will be running on empty just when you need energy the most.

> Breakfast is a key part of your tournament preparation. Without a good breakfast, you'll be running on empty by the late rounds. (Eating too much is just as bad.) If you're too nervous to eat, go for a walk to calm your nerves.

Eating too much is just as bad. I've seen some fencers stuffing themselves with ketchup-drenched sausages and potatoes for breakfast. As a result, they were too full to move and lost their bouts in the pools, even though their level was much higher than that.

Some fencers have tournament jitters—they're afraid to lose. The result is that they can't eat anything at all. The nervousness is natural, but they still need energy! In this case I'd advise my teammates to go for a walk outside. You have to get some fresh air. It's better to go with a teammate than to walk by yourself. You can have an easy conversation, which will help to relax your mind. I'm sure after an easy morning walk, you'll eat something and get at least some of the energy you need.

Good preparation also includes nourishment *during* the competition.

Good preparation includes nourishment during the competition as well. Many fencers eat very little or nothing at all. Some of them drink sodas or juice, which is also wrong.

You lose a lot of liquid during a long competition. You have to refill your body with water—rehydrate—and replace the lost minerals as well, if the competition lasts for a long time. I used to drink natural water (still, not sparkling), as well as energy drinks.

What else is good to eat during a competition? I used to eat chocolate, bananas, cereal bars or cookies—in other words, carbohydrates for energy.

Very often I had to leave my hotel for the competition before they'd served breakfast. For such cases, I'd buy some yogurt, bananas etc. the night before. I always had a little immersion heater with me. I'd make some tea or coffee for myself and go to the fencing hall.

It all adds up to this: *a strong body means a strong mind!*

So try to help yourself out!

Here's an example of what happens when these principles go wrong…

Our first opponent in the team event was Russia. They had two finalists from the individual event, but they weren't fresh and ready the way we were. We beat them and advanced to the final eight against Hungary, who had beaten us just a few weeks earlier in Cape Town. They fell to us 45 – 33.

To be sure of a medal, we next needed to get past a very strong Chinese team. I had never seen my teammates rise to the occasion the way they did this time. Usually, all the pressure was on my shoulders: I'd need to score 20 – 25 touches for us to have a chance. This time, everyone fenced solidly and securely.

One strange incident punctuated the match. The fencing hall was stocked with free drinks for the athletes: the Aquarius energy drink, plus Coke and Fanta. For many people, free stuff is sacred: it's a religious obligation to take as much as you can—or more.

I kept telling my teammates that commercial soda is no good for you while you're fencing: the combination of too much acid and too much sugar is no good for the digestion. But Oleg Matseichuk had his own vision of such things. He kept loading up.

Right in the middle of his last bout, he asked the referee to stop the bout. While the referee was still asking him what the matter was, Oleg went to the end of the strip and puked a orange liquid of a truly unearthly, industrial hue.

But nothing could stop us. We won the match, 45 – 36.

There were a few hours of rest before the final. We understood that we had a good chance of winning. At some point, I think, the feeling came over each of us that this was one of the most important days of our career. I know that it felt that way to me.

We were fencing the Cubans, who had come with their first team: Elvis Gregory and Rolando Tucker, perennially two of the world's best, and Raúl Perojo, a rising star who would be a finalist in the World Championships the following year. It was a World Championship caliber team that looked on paper to be far stronger than Ukraine.

The match took place in the open air, which is disorienting to most fencers, since the light is much brighter and all the distances seem different outside the confines of an enclosed space. My father decided to get there and warm up early so that we could adjust to these conditions. When we started our calisthenics, the Cubans hadn't arrived. Only after we began the fencing part of our warm-up did the Cubans show up, laughing, joking, and relaxed. They couldn't imagine losing to us.

Their mistake. After the first three bouts, we led 15 – 5!

I called my boys together and told them to hang on.

"Just score five touches in each bout," I said. "You can lose 7 – 5, 8 – 5; it's OK. Just get us five touches closer."

Then it would be my turn again and we would regain the lead. I beat Perojo and Gregory, 5 – 0 and 5 – 1, and when I came up against Tucker in the last bout, we were leading 40 – 35. I didn't want to wait for his mistakes this time. I put him under intense pressure, trying to take away any possibility for him to attack. That day he had no chance. We won, 45 – 38, beating one of the strongest teams in the world by seven touches.

It was a great victory for Ukraine, and an even greater achievement for my father.

At the end of August, I received the "Order of the President of Ukraine" from the hands of the Prime Minister.

Attack into Preparation—Don't Call This a Counterattack!
(Photo by G. Minozzi)

My First World Championship Gold: Cape Town, 1997
(photo by G. Minozzi)

The Championship Streak

1997—1998

Meanwhile, I had been acquiring all the necessary documents to be able to work in the Netherlands: working permit, medical insurance, and so on. My coaching jobs in Holland and Austria had been, strictly speaking, illegal. Now I could work without feeling like a criminal.

I was coaching the two top Dutch foilists: a woman, Indra Angad-Gaur, and a man, Paul Sanders. My job was to improve their world ranking, and I'm glad to say that I succeeded in a relatively short time. In addition, there were other fencers trying to compete internationally at the cadet and junior levels. Finally, I coached a group of kids who were fencing "just for fun." I was paid by the Dutch Olympic Committee and the OKK Fencing Club in The Hague. My salaries added up to about $1300 a month. (In addition, of course, I was still a member of the Ukrainian team, which paid for my own competition expenses.) Even taking account of my private lessons, it wasn't much to live on.

My job would be to coach and travel around the world with the Dutch women's foil team; meanwhile I had to find the time to train and travel for myself. I didn't have much time for rest. I didn't gain weight by switching from

Ukrainian cuisine to Dutch—in fact, I lost a few pounds, down to 78 kilograms (just under 172 pounds), my lowest since 1990.

Without proper preparation, I plunged into the 1997 – 98 competitive season. After winning a small competition in Belgium, it was time for the European Championships, this year held in Gdansk, Poland.

I was badly out of shape in this event, and I started to lose strength in the pools. In direct elimination, I really started to suffer, losing all finesse and mobility. After losing to me 15 – 11, one fencer thanked me for not beating him worse. I thought, "If you knew how I was feeling, you might have had a good chance of beating me."

In order to make it to the final four, I beat Ralf Bissdorf on will and nerve alone. I felt so bad that I hated myself. In the semis, I trailed Jean-Noël Ferrari of France throughout the bout, gasping for breath like a fish out of water. With a minute left, Jean-Noël led 14 – 11. With only seconds to go, I tied the score at 14-all. The coin toss went my way, and I had the priority for the final minute. That meant that Ferrari had to score to win and I didn't. Half-dead, I let the clock run down, calculated the moment when he had to attack, and won with a parry-riposte.

> With priority in my favor, I let the clock run down, calculated when he had to attack, and won with a riposte.

My opponent in the final was Adam Krzesinski of Poland, a 6'5" left-hander like Shevchenko. We used to joke that he and Shevchenko were twin brothers separated at birth. I had trained with the Polish team several times, and this helped the Polish foilists find some keys to my fencing.

(It's always useful to train with stronger fencers: you gain insight into their timing and repertoire; your fear of them slowly but surely evaporates, and your coach can give you tactical insights that you might not figure out for yourself.)

Using his knowledge of my fencing, combined with my near-exhaustion and his strong desire, Adam burst into an early lead, and I had to play catch-up throughout the match. The result was that my European Championship passed to Adam in a close bout, 15 – 13.

Nevertheless, at some point during my losing effort, I started to feel happy. I was proud that I could win bouts on strength of will alone. On a day that was absolutely not my day, when the physical and technical odds were against me, I could still mount the podium.

I thought, "I am becoming a real 'Highlander,' an immortal. I am near the peak of my fencing career."

My life that year was one of nonstop travel. Let me show you my itinerary.

Just as a coach, I went to Hungary, Germany, Italy, Russia, Germany again, Austria, Argentina and the USA.

As a fencer *and* coach, I went to Belgium, Poland, Cuba, France, Bulgaria and Switzerland.

Just as a fencer, I went to Austria, Russia, France, Italy, Hungary and Germany.`

With this rhythm, I could neither rest nor train. All I could do was coach, travel, and fence.

Every morning, I'd drive from Rotterdam to the The Hague, give two or three lessons, and then drive home for lunch and a few hours of rest. Evenings, I'd supervise the kids' practice and then work with the fencers who were looking to improve their level. Sometimes, for my own training, I would play soccer or fence with them. A week before my own competitions, I'd do some running and fence a little. It wasn't enough, but it was all I had time for. I wasn't happy when I didn't win at World Cup events, but somehow, I didn't care that much either. I was trying to fence for the public, stay in shape, and have fun.

In the final of the Lion of Bonn, I led Young Ho Kim 10 – 2 but he beat me 15 – 13, taking revenge on me for his defeat in the World Championships, and showing his tremendous potential as a foilist.

The next weekend, I was with the Ukrainian team for the Seven Nations tournament. The team had a respectable result—fourth out of eight teams (Ukraine had been added to the original seven), and I won individually.

The European Confederation had created a strange schedule that year. They added a second European Championships in Plovdiv, Bulgaria to end the regular season. That wasn't so bad. But the FIE had scheduled the World Championships in La Chaux-de-Fonds, Switzerland, in October, about three months later. That meant that the fencers could neither take a real vacation, because we'd get out of shape, but we couldn't train very hard either, because then we'd arrive at the Worlds too tired. They probably had their own good reasons for the scheduling, but it was hard on the competitors.

Plovdiv was not a city of triumph for me. Ralf Bissdorf beat me badly in the quarters, 15 – 11, leaving me in fifth place.

One memorable incident at that tournament presented a real moral dilemma. Two Austrians were fighting each other for a place in the final four: Michael Ludwig and my friend Benny Wendt. Despite receiving a yellow card, Benny had a comfortable lead, 10 – 2. By all rights, he should have closed out the bout without any drama, but sport is sport, and Michael Ludwig started to fight for every touch, one hard-fought touch at a time. He was closing the gap, but not quickly enough, it seemed, because the score reached 14 – 9 for Benny. Surely the outcome was no longer in doubt.

But now Michael started to read Benny like a first-grader's storybook. His score advanced: 10...11...12...13...14 – 14!

Everything hung in the balance.

Back before the bout started, when the fencers were called to the strip, Benny Wendt hadn't been ready. He made a mistake as he hurried to the strip: he forgot to put on his plastron as the rules require. The referee made a mistake, as well. He was supposed to check for plastrons at the start of the bout, as the rules require. He didn't, and the bout proceeded.

Put yourself in Michael Ludwig's place. You noticed that your teammate didn't put his plastron on. You can make the final four of the European Championship, *just by asking the referee to check your opponent's plastron!* Since he already has a yellow card, the result will be a penalty touch and a win for you...*at the price of informing on your teammate.*

> Would you rat out your teammate to get into the finals of a World Cup?

What would you do to make the final four of the Europeans? What if it were the finals of the World Championships? What would you do?

Michael Ludwig had made his decision. He asked the referee to look under Benny's jacket. He made the final four.

In my eyes, he was totally wrong. In that situation, I would want the outcome of the match to be decided by fencing.

I spent July in Holland, playing soccer and doing some running. I wanted to stop fencing for a while so I would get hungry for it.

In August, I started to train harder, working hard on the athletic aspects of fencing. I was mostly doing footwork and hitting the target. I didn't start actually fencing until a week before the Steglitzer Pokal tournament in Berlin that September. I was nowhere near my best at that tournament (which I won) but I felt strong physically. I was mentally alert too, taking note of my opponent's mistakes—and my own.

In late September, taking my students with me, I went to Kiev to spend some time with my daughter and train with my father for the World Championships.

Dad didn't load my training very heavily, but for the first three days I was completely out of it. I had lost the habit and the appetite for two-a-day training sessions. My legs were too heavy and my arm movements too big. I looked more like a mediocre tennis player than a good fencer. On the fourth day, though, things finally clicked, and I started to feel like a fencer again.

Naturally, at that point, I got injured—a muscle pull in my left thigh. Every lunge I made sent me a painful message, which I stupidly ignored. I kept telling myself that time was too short for me to cut back on training. Fortunately, my father saw this and changed the schedule, forcing me to rest.

I felt ready to defend my World Championship. But would my injury permit it?

After just a few individual lessons with my father, I felt that my skills were at their peak. I was ready to fight for a place on the podium at the Worlds. The question was whether my injury would permit it.

On the first of October, I flew back to Holland. On Sunday the fourth, I boarded the train for La Chaux-de-Fonds. The direct elimination from 64 was scheduled for Wednesday the seventh. My World Cup results for the year hadn't been great, but they had been good enough to get me a first-day bye. I felt good that I had done that well with so little training, but I was nervous about defending my championship.

La Chaux-de-Fonds is a small city near the French border, famous for its watch making industry. We got off the train and checked into our quarters, a local youth hostel.

The room reminded me of a railroad sleeping car: a tiny room with four double-decker bunk beds. We had nowhere to stow our fencing gear, and I spent a restless night in an uncomfortable upper bunk.

The next morning, I took a lesson from my father. It was a great lesson to have before a competition: one of those "perfect," high-level lessons that stretch you and at the same time make you feel good about your form and your ability. I went to the fencing site the next day to give my student a lesson and my father wanted to give me another lesson right afterwards. This time, I said no, I was worried that a little bit too much training would spoil my "perfecto."

Tuesday, the night before the competition, I took a look at the direct elimination table, as I did whenever I got the chance. Personally, I liked to know the name of my first opponent and to imagine my probable path to the final bout. I would think about each possible opponent, his strengths and weaknesses; I'd make a preliminary plan for each bout. The advantage I got from this mental rehearsal outweighed whatever worry I may have felt.

This year's table certainly worried me. I showed it to my father, saying "What a backbreaker!"

In my half of the draw were Oscar Garcia Perez and Rolando Tucker of Cuba (Garcia was a steady team medalist for the Cubans), Alessandro Puccini of Italy, Ralf Bissdorf and Wolfgang Wienand of Germany, Dmitri Shevchenko of Russia, Haibin Wang and Dong Zhaozhi of China, and Lionel Plumenail. It was an all-star team of opponents. Tomorrow was going to be a hard day.

I slept well that night. When I got up in the morning, I had stopped worrying about defending my title. All I wanted to do was to be ready for today. I hoped that the first bout would tell me.

It didn't tell me as much as I wanted it to. I beat the Egyptian Foulad with ease, 15 – 6, but I wasn't happy with my fencing. I couldn't fool my body. By the middle of the bout I was breathing hard. I had to fight myself to stay active. I was resolved not to show my fatigue and weakness to anyone, but my father saw it.

My next opponent was the lefthander, Dong, who had beaten me in Athens in '94 with his great footwork and superb feeling for distance. I would need a strong start to beat him, because I didn't think I could come from behind.

I motored out to a 7 – 0 lead, but burned a lot of energy in the process. I wished that I had an oxygen mask. Dong kept getting closer and closer, but I hung on to win 15 – 12, running on fumes by the end. I felt like a Lamborghini that had run out of gas in the middle of the desert.

My father had no way of helping me. I saw his worry and pain, but I was the one on the strip, defending not only my title, but my honor. (That's the way I was thinking about it—I felt that it would be a disgrace if I went out of the tournament too early.)

Next was Zsolt Ersek, who had shared a team bronze for Hungary at the 1988 Olympics. He was a surprise winner over Lionel Plumenail and Haibin Wang.

It wasn't a pretty bout: there were delays, technical problems, and a million or so off-target hits. Half-alive, I floundered to a 15 – 9 win.

Wolfgang Wienand had finished his bout a long time earlier, and had rested up for 20 – 30 minutes watching my struggles. With only a minimal break, I had to fence him— for the final four and a place on the podium. Wienand had beaten me a few times—once in the final of a World Cup in St. Petersburg in 1996; more recently in a World Cup in Portugal. He was full of confidence; I was full of hope.

At the beginning of the bout, Wienand seemed to know my moves before I made them, as if he was reading from a book that described how the bout would go. At the break, he led 7 – 1.

I could see the pain on my father's face as he tried to cheer me up; I could read the pitying looks on my teammates' faces. They felt as if I had already lost. And when I went back onto the strip at the end of the minute's break, I have to say that I felt the same way.

But I realized what I was feeling, and a weight fell from my shoulders: I was no longer burdened by having to defend my title, preserve my honor, even to achieve any particular result. For the first time all day, I was myself again.

My Lamborghini now had a full tank of gas, and it developed that Wienand had read only half the book on our bout. I outscored him 14 – 4 to win the bout 15 – 11.

There was a little time to rest up before the semis. Elvis Gregory was paired with young Salvatore "Toti" Sanzo of Italy (the 1995 Junior World Cup winner, future World Champion in 2001 and 2004 Olympic Silver Medalist), while I would face 36-year-old Piotr Kielpikowski, a two-time Olympic team medalist for Poland. My father and I walked to the hall where the finals would be held, so we could relax and warm up. I wasn't feeling tired any more. (At this point in the competition, everyone is tired but still full of energy. You know that you have at least a bronze medal in your hands. You can get more, but not less!)

It's possible that you can be too happy at this point just because you have the bronze. I think that's what happened with Piotr: he wasn't hungry for the gold, and I beat him 15 – 8.

One touch from this bout stands out in my memory: I attacked deep—maybe too deep, because, as I watched, Piotr made his parry and began his riposte. His blade moved inexorably toward my chest. The only thing I could think of was to fall down backwards like a professional wrestler. His point missed me by centimeters.

The problem with this tactic is that it merits a yellow card for fencing out of control. I started waving my legs in the air like a dying insect. Waves of laughter filled the hall, and the referee, joining in, withheld his warning.

Elvis Gregory had beaten Toti Sanzo in the first semifinal and was waiting for me in the final. That was fine

> The pressue was off me. I didn't care about the World Championship any more. I just wanted to fence a good bout.

with me. In fact, everything was fine with me. I didn't care about the final result. I can't explain why, but all the pressure was off me. It was good just to have made the final. I just wanted to put on a good show for the spectators...and to fence a good bout.

Elvis was the overall World Cup winner that year. Since the great Mauro Numa in 1985, no one had won the overall World Cup and the World Championship in the same year. I had won the World Cup in four consecutive years, but was never World Champion. Before the Championships, I had given an interview in which I was bold enough to say that Elvis wouldn't win the Championship because of the "burden" of being the World Cup winner.

Of course, Elvis had his own thoughts on the matter. He had never won an Olympics or World Championships. This might be the day he had been working for and dreaming about for many years. Whichever way you looked at it, it was number one in the world versus number two—the World Cup winner versus the defending World Champion.

The score stood at 5 – 5 when Elvis advanced to the attack. I ducked and extended my arm in a stop-thrust. Just as my point arrived, I felt a click—not the touch, but my left knee. It seemed so loud that I was sure that everyone in the hall had heard it.. Then came the pain. I could barely put my foot down, even on tiptoe. I asked the referee for medical attention, but he refused. I asked again, and got not only a refusal, but a yellow card. I would have to tough it out until the break, hoping not to fall too far behind.

Elvis pressed me hard, trying to turn the tide of the bout, but his pressure worked in my favor. I went to the break with a 9 – 7 advantage.

The only thing that could be done for me during the one-minute break was to freeze my knee. That helped a lot, plus Elvis slowed down a bit, and I made three touches in a row: 12 – 7. Elvis took the next touch and it was 12 – 8.

I attacked, Elvis parried. Closing to escape his riposte, I stepped on his foot. With the yellow card I already had for trying to get a medical halt, my offence would mean a red card and the loss of a touch.

Most people would have taken their foot off Elvis. What would you have done?

I froze in position, keeping my foot on Elvis. He looked meaningfully at the referee. I looked meaningfully at the referee, too, pressing my palms together beseechingly. Then I hugged Elvis. Just as before, against Kielpikowski, I heard that wave of forgiving laughter in the hall. Somehow, I didn't get the red card.

I decided to go on the defensive and take advantage of Elvis's mistakes. But he quit making them, becoming excruciatingly precise and touching me five times in a row to even the score at 12 – 12. Obviously, there was nothing to be gained by defense. I attacked and scored. 13 – 12: Elvis attacked and scored: 13 – 13.

> I decided to go on the defensive and take advantage of his mistakes. But he quit making them and tied the

I decided to trust to the luck of the attack. I scored twice with attacks to pull the match out, 15 – 13.

I had defended my World Championship. It was the first victory that my father could watch all the way. He was next to the strip during every bout.

An hour later, after the press conference and the doping control, my knee hurt so badly that I had to ask for help carrying my fencing bag, and I couldn't sleep that night because of the pain. The next day, a German physiotherapist told me that I had a partially torn meniscus.

"You were lucky," he said with a slight smile. "You tore it in the last bout. Any earlier in the competition, you couldn't have continued."

1998—1999

The 1998—99 season would begin for me in January and end at the World Championships in Seoul, South Korea, at the start of September. I also took on some extra work, giving individual lessons once a week in Breda, 60 km south of Rotterdam.

I also began to train some fencers, actually the best young male and female fencers in the Netherlands.

As I said in the Prologue, there's a difference between giving lessons and being what we call a trainer. The trainer is in charge of the athlete's total training: lessons are an important part of the total picture, but only a part. For example, I was able to create a strong competitive group for my fencers, guaranteeing good sparring, which is also very important. And I had to direct the buildup for competitions, and the pre-competition routine, as well as coaching at the competitions themselves.

That year I went to fifteen international women's tournaments, traveling to the USA, Argentina, China, South Korea, and Russia, as well as countries closer to Holland; and in addition, I had to accompany my younger students to regional tournaments.

My schedule as trainer and coach ate up most of my time, leaving me no time for fencing. All I could do was play soccer for twenty minutes almost every evening. I was in decent shape physically—I just wasn't fencing.

> There's a difference between just giving lessons and being a real trainer.

214

Ready or not, as January came to an end, the time approached for my favorite World Cup. This event has gone by many names over the years: the Martini-Rossi, the Martini, the Fabergé, and, as I write, the CIP, the Challenge International de Paris. Sometimes I felt that this was an unlucky event for me—I would lose in the round of 32, and always on the same unlucky strip! Once, I went to the DT (Directoire Technique, the event officials) and asked them to put me on a different strip. They agreed, but a few minutes later I was called to the same strip! I blew up, went to the DT again and *demanded* a new strip. (And would you believe I got it?)

Win or lose, though, I loved this tournament because it gave a rare opportunity to fence before a knowledgeable crowd of almost 5,000. Sometimes you hear people say that fencing doesn't attract crowds the way it used to. Paris was always an exception. And I think that with the right promotion, fencing could draw crowds more widely. Perhaps it could be like golf or tennis, if not like basketball or soccer.

Every year since 1995, I had made the final eight in Paris. Though I had never won, I loved the feeling of fencing before so many spectators, trying to fence beautifully (to delight the spectators) as well as to win.

This year I made it to the finals after a tough semifinal bout over Elvis Gregory, coming from four touches behind to win, 15 – 14. While I was trying to get my head together before the final, I was accosted by a man whose face was vaguely familiar to me. He started to tell me what an artist I was for having handed Elvis the lead, creating a drama, and then winning with ease (in *his* opinion) at the end. Then he started to tell me his own sports experiences…

I recognized him: he had formerly been Ukraine's Minister of International Affairs. Now he was Ambassador to France. He was still talking. Now he was

The Paris International Challenge unfolds before a knowledgeable crowd of almost 5,000 spectators.

teaching me how to fence.

Fortunately, just then the chief of the Ukrainian fencing delegation came to talk to me. I whispered to him to keep the Ambassador away from me.

I lost to Oscar Garcia Perez in an even bout. Probably the Ambassador thought that it was because I didn't take his advice. In reality, it was because of errors by the referee of a kind that was all too common: not recognizing an attack on preparation. Just because a fencer is marching down the strip, it doesn't mean that he is attacking!

The next World Cup was in Venice, another city where I loved to fence because of the beauty of the architecture and the fine weather. The sports palace is a gem, especially the lower gym, which is actually underwater. I won, taking my sixteenth World Cup victory. Now Andrea Borella's record of seventeen was in reach, and I wanted to break it.

The goal was elusive. That season, I finished second in Vienna and third in Havana and Teheran. That didn't get me any closer to Borella, but it did put me neck and neck with Wolfgang Wienand for the overall World Cup title for the year. I headed for Haifa, Israel, for the final event, the one that would determine the winner. As was my habit, I was trying to calculate all the possible variations of our results: if I went out in the round of the sixteen, how far would he have to advance to beat me?

But Wolfgang didn't show up. I would be the overall World Cup winner for the fifth time in my career—the record in men's foil—without even fencing for it.

But I did fence the tournament—and won it, tying Borella's record.

As the last event of my regular season, I fenced in the "Super-Master" gala event in Padova (Padua), Italy. It was a splendid occasion. As part of it we wore the new-design masks with see-through visors. They were supplied by the

British fencing supplier, Leon Paul. They'd be the source of a surprise for me at next year's World Championships in Seoul.

The Super Master event was significant for me in another way. It was organized by the Fencing Club of Conegliano, Italy, whose president, Sergio Santarossa, had founded the Viktoria line of fencing equipment. Sergio proposed a sponsorship contract with me, and I agreed to use and promote the Viktoria products. Later, Sergio and Conegliano became even more important to me, when he invited me to live and coach there. But I'm getting ahead of the story...

After the Super-Masters, I flew to Kiev with a few of my students to prepare, as usual, for the World Championships.

My father met me at the airport with a surprise message: the Mayor of Kiev had invited me to a reception he was holding in an hour's time. The head of the Kiev Sport Committee had arranged for a car with a driver to take me direct to City Hall. I even got a bouquet! I was touched to know that my hometown dignitaries were recognizing me.

Beyond that, my father told me, we were about to resolve my "apartment problem." In both the old USSR and its successors, housing was a very scarce and precious commodity. New construction was far short of what was needed, so families crowded together in the existing apartments, and a new apartment might cost $20 – 30,000, far beyond my means with my $200 monthly salary. We elite athletes didn't have to worry so much—my silver medal from the 1992 Olympics got me the privilege of buying an apartment at the "state price" of $500 – 700. But of course I lost that apartment on my divorce: my ex-wife and daughter needed it.

In 1997, during the banquet after I received the Order of the President of Ukraine, the Prime Minister told me that he would see what could be done for me. Within six months, I heard that an apartment was in the works. Just before the 1998 World Championships, the head of the Kiev Sport Committee told me that if I won, the apartment would me mine. I won my second championship in a row and continued to hear promises.

Now I was a guest of honor, riding from the airport to the Mayor's reception. Too late I found out that the "reception," held a few days before the presidential elections, was a rally of "Athletes for the Re-election of President Kuchma!" I was there along with the rhythmic gymnastics star Elena Vitrichenko and the hockey player Dmitri Khristich, who played for thirteen years in the NHL. Elena, who had stayed in Kiev, explained the situation to Dmitri and me, who were clueless: we were supposed to make the people at the reception (and the following press conference) believe that we enthusiastically supported the policies of President Kuchma and wanted him reelected for another five-year term.

I was boiling mad, but didn't feel that I had much of a choice. Everything seemed to go smoothly, but at the press conference, the last question floored us all.

A journalist asked all of us, "Has any of you actually read Kuchma's platform? Do you know what his policies are?" We stood there stunned. All I could feel was shame. We were lying, not just to these journalists, but to the whole Ukrainian people.

Elena nudged me and whispered, "Sergei, say something!" What could I say? But I did.

Five days later, the Head of the Sports Committee told me that, yes, I would be getting an apartment… *if* I won *this* year's World Championships (for the *third* straight time! Oh, yes…and *if* the Ukrainian foil team qualified for the 2000 Olympics at these same Championships. That was all.

This was my reward for being tricked into selling myself. Thanks. You can imagine how I felt.

It was exactly a year and ten days since I'd had my last lesson with my father. In the next twelve days, I had to get back to basics, relearn forgotten reactions, and try to get into top physical shape for the most important tournament of the year. Since my theory was that the overall World Cup winner (me) wasn't going to win the World Championships anyway, I tried to think about the actual result as little as possible. In any case, I had another goal: to help my team as much as possible to qualify for the Sydney Olympics. We needed to make the top eight, which hadn't happened since 1994.

Flying from Holland, I arrived at the Seoul, the World Championships city, a little before the Ukrainian team, which was flying from Kiev. After we finished our greetings, they told me that they'd heard on the radio that I'd been given an apartment. I knew immediately what was up: the opposition was circulating this rumor that the apartment was the payment for my press conference performance. It was unfortunately true, except for one detail: there was no apartment!

At the venue, I stopped by the Leon Paul fencing equipment display. Naturally, the stand was full of pictures promoting their latest equipment. In fact, there was even a picture of me, wearing the Leon Paul mask with the new Lexan visor at the Super-Master gala last year! So I was advertising Leon Paul equipment. Wait a minute—who had asked me?

Barry Paul couldn't understand my protest—no fencer had ever complained before. I told him that he'd be hearing from my attorney shortly and walked off.

Saying that was one thing. Now I had to find an attorney. Fortunately, Yann Bernard, a Canadian fencer at the Championships, was a lawyer back in Canada when he wasn't fencing. A few minutes after I described the situation to him, he was representing my interests.

Six months later I got a check for US $500.00 from Leon Paul. It's not a huge sum, but I think that it was important to show fencers that they have rights.

It's not that I have a war with Leon Paul—quite the contrary. Two years later, I signed a contract with them in which I agreed to give them the right to use my name and image to market their products, and they agreed to manufacture a special "Golubitsky Pro" blade and a Golubitsky grip, to my design and specifications. The firm of Leon Paul is now my sponsor.

The "Golubitsky Pro" blades are made exactly the way I like them, with the weight back toward the hand and maximum flexibility near the tip.

The handles, which fine-tune the Belgian grip, are designed for precision control. The thumb rest is flat and wide, and the vertical piece between the thumb and forefinger slopes away so that the thumb can rest naturally. The little "trigger" projection between the middle and fourth fingers is bigger than what you find on most handles so that these fingers gain greater control. Finally, the fencer gets a choice of thicknesses on the main downward projection, where the last two fingers go. I used to use tape for this, but Leon Paul has substituted rubber collars, which give a controlled feedback that allows even greater precision and significant fatigue reduction.

I now have a fine relationship with the firm of Leon Paul, so everything turned out for the best.

I have a similarly fine relationship with Viktoria and wear the beautiful fencing shoes they make. On the next two pages, you'll see the result of my collaboration with Leon Paul and Viktoria.

1999 World Championships—Seoul

I had arrived in Seoul on the twenty-ninth of October. Soon enough it was November 3, the day of the foil

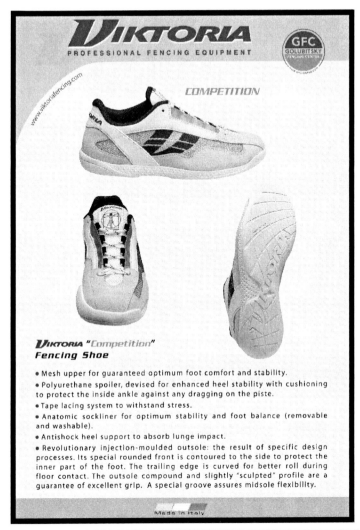

My Sponsors—Viktoria Fencing Shoes

Viktoria's founder, Sergio Santarossa, sponsored the Padova Super Masters' Tournament, where I agreed to endorse his fencing shoes. I fenced in these shoes for the last two years of my career, and I loved them. They have a mesh top that's comfortable and fits well, a polyurethane heel cup for maximum protection, and a really beautiful anatomical sole for perfect balance and traction. Later, Sergio invited me to live and coach in his home town of Conegliano. Now Daniel Boles and I plan to bring this product to America.

Leon Paul

GOLUBITSKY-PRO RANGE

Golubitsky and Leon Paul Forging a better sword.

The Blade: "In order to maintain perfect control you need balance. The blade needs more weight towards the hand and the flexibility at the tip. That's why I designed the Golubitsky-Pro® Blade." Sergei

The Grip: "You need maximum positive contact with the hand and as all fencers are different we designed the first adjustable grip. The Golubitsky-Pro® handle is based on the grip I used to win 3 World Championships but with an adjustable rubber element so you can control the balance, comfort and feel of your weapon." Sergei

See them both at www.leonpaul.com

My Sponsors—Leon Paul Fencing Equipment

L eon Paul and I started off with the threat of a lawsuit, but now we are partners. They make the Golubitsky Pro blade and grip to my exact specifications.

individuals. I was completely aware of the burden on my shoulders. If I won, I'd be the first male fencer ever to win three consecutive World Championships (not counting the Olympics). I'd be the last champion of the twentieth century (if you count the beginning and end of the century the way most people do!). I'd be the first male foil fencer since 1985 to win the overall World Cup and the World Championship in the same year—and get that particular monkey off my back after four consecutive overall World Cups and two consecutive World Championships—but no Cup and Championship in the same year. And just maybe, if the Ukrainian team fenced well and the authorities were to be trusted, I'd wind up with an apartment of my own.

I was motivated, all right. And for the first time in many years, I was coming up to a major competition without injuries. I was feeling more or less ready to rock.

My first bout, against the Hungarian Bence Juhasz, should have been an opportunity to get my mind and body into a groove, but instead it was a nail-biter, a war of nerves, like epee. After the first three minutes, the score was only 3 – 1; after six minutes, it had only reached 6 – 4, my favor. Finally, in the third period, as things heated up under time pressure, I began to move better, winning 15 – 9 with ten seconds to go. I wasn't happy with my fencing yet; I anticipated a tough day at the office.

The next bout, with Benny Wendt, almost strained our friendship. Despite a yellow card, I was leading comfortably 13 – 6 in the third period, when he threw his foil and hit me, the way Shevchenko had in Cape Town. I don't think that friends should do that to each other. I was so mad at Benny that I started to scream at the referee. Red card. Two touches against me on the same action. Still too angry to fence properly, I let the bout get close.

At 14 – 12, there was poetic justice. Benny forced a corps á corps and got a red card to lose the bout.

I screamed at the referee and got a red card—two touches against me on the same action!

To get to the final of eight, I had to beat Cliff Bayer of the US, coached by the Ukrainian Yefim Litwan. He was the only American at that time to have won two World Cups, and on his way to victory in St. Petersburg, he had beaten me in the quarterfinals. I found out later that his coach had kept telling him, "Fence the way Golubitsky does!"

Having beaten me once gave him confidence, and he started out very strong. In no time, I was down 4 – 0. Then my inner "Highlander" woke up. In the remainder of the bout, I scored fifteen touches to his four.

Next came the very strong Rolando Tucker. Our bout drew the attention of many coaches and fencers. They audience tightened my focus and made me fence well. I won by the score of 15 – 8 to enter the final four.

A few hours later, I was taking a lesson from my father in the hall where the fencers were warming up for the finals. Across the way, Wolfgang Wienand, my destined opponent, was warming up with his coach. I felt tight and nervous, remembering how Wienand had jumped out to a 7 – 1 lead on me a year previously.

Dad pointed across the hall to where Wolfgang was warming up. "Look at *him*," he told me. "He looks *really* scared."

Just before the finals, the World Cup presentation ceremony took place. The legendary French fencer Christian D'Oriola presented the trophy to me.

D'Oriola had begun his career in the era of visually judged, non-electric foil, winning the World Championships in 1947 and '49, winning the Olympics in '52 and the Championships again in '53, and '54, not to mention taking silver in the '48 Olympics and the '55 World Championships. He was the dominant fencer of his age, but what would happen with the introduction of the heavier and differently balanced electric foil at the 1956 Olympics? D'Oriola gave a decisive answer, winning the gold but quitting the sport in disgust over the clumsiness of the new weapon. (He returned long enough to take sixth at the 1960 Olympics.) In short, this man was one of the greatest fencers of the twentieth century.

Now he was shaking my hand. "I am a fan of yours," he was telling me, "a fan of your fencing."

It was one of the highest compliments I have ever received.

In the first semifinal, Matteo Zennaro beat Young Ho Kim by one touch. That was good news for me, since Kim had worried me. Now, if I could just get past Wienand, I had a good shot at the gold.

I was prepared for the bout of my life, but it didn't happen. Maybe Wienand's defeat at last year's Championships was still on his mind. He wasn't ready that day. The score was 15 – 3. I was in the finals.

Now it was Matteo's turn.

I will never forget what my father once told me: "Victory is easy; it's the road to victory that's hard."

I had been down the road. This bout wasn't easier or harder than many, many others I had fenced. It wasn't dramatic or spectacular. Matteo got as close as 8 – 8, but I ground out a victory, 15 – 12.

I became only the fourth fencer in history to win three consecutive World Championships, even counting the Olympics.

> My father had told me: "Victory is easy. It is *the road to victory* that's hard."

The FIE Magazine *Escrime* wrote about me,

> *"In these circumstances, he had no need to stretch his talents. Golubitsky comes onto the piste, comes on guard, advances or retires, feints or doesn't play cat and mouse, shakes hands with his opponent and the referee, comes back to collect his medal (gold, inevitably) - and goes back to giving lessons to the Dutch team. "*

They make it sound so easy, don't they?

But I remember what my father told me after my first title, in 1997. I was exultant: "I'm World Champion this year!"

"You are the champion *today*," he told me. "Tomorrow, you have to prove it again."

I felt strange the next day. The previous two years, I had been exultant. Now I felt...good. Not great...just good. It was weird.

Two days later, I helped the Ukrainian foil team qualify for the 2000 Olympics in Sydney, beating out the US for a spot in the top eight. We had done it against the odds.

Just to get ahead of the story a little, however: I didn't get that apartment.

I went off to Sydney to rest up for the new Olympic year.

A year that I would curse.

Winners of Three Consecutive World Championships

George Piller, (Hungary, Men's Sabre)
1930, '31, '32 (Olympics)

Ilona Elek, (Hungary, Women's Foil)
1934, '35, '36 (Olympics)

Christian d'Oriola (France, Men's Foil)
1952 (Olympics), '53, '54

Sergei Golubitsky (Ukraine, Men's Foil)
1997, '98, '99

Valentinal Vezzali (Italy, Women's Foil)
1999, 2000 (Olympics), 2001

The End Begins

1999—2000: The Year of Troubles

As soon as I returned from Sydney, I started to get massive stomach pains, just as I had the year before. I went to the doctor and asked whether I had some sort of virus. He sent me for a blood test and gave me some medicine. The blood tests were negative and the medicine worked. I was happy until I found out that I had an ulcer. This was the first, and the least, of my problems in this year of troubles.

Once again, I had no time to train. As the trainer of my junior fencers, I was already in the middle of the season. As the trainer of my senior fencers, I was at the very beginning. I was on two schedules.

As a trainer, then, I traveled to Hungary and Germany in late January. Then, after only a few training sessions (which I had to force myself to fence!) I went to the CIP Tournament in Paris, the opener of the 2000 men's foil circuit. I surprised myself by making the final eight with so little practice. I guess my experience counted: the sum of all my past training and competition gave me the ability to read my opponents and react coolly in critical moments.

In the quarterfinals I encountered Roman Christen. We had known each other for years. He's two years older than I am and was on the German team at the 1989 World

Championships in Denver. He hadn't had the greatest results, but his steady training at Tauberbischofsheim, one of the strongest training centers in the world, brought him to a level which occasionally gave him fine results. In 1992, for example, he'd won a Peugeot automobile at a strong competition in France. I didn't figure he was going to make the German Olympic team, but making the quarters of this Grand Prix tournament had certainly given him a foot in the door.

An hour before we fenced, he tried some mind games. "I hate fencing you—you are too slow for me," he said.

I laughed. He knew and I knew that for him to beat me, something really extraordinary was going to have to happen.

As I said, my stomach problems were only the beginning of my nightmare that season. So something extraordinary happened.

It started like a fantasy. The announcer gave me a great introduction: Mr. Fencing! The big French crowd erupted in cheers. I was loving it.

And then I was fencing beautifully: making elegant touches, cracking jokes, having a ball in front of the biggest crowd in the world of fencing.

With the score 6 – 4 in my favor, I made a counterattack without proper preparation. Roman took a hard opposition and touched me: a fine touch for him, making the score 6 – 5.

But he had jammed my wrist, and the pain was excruciating. I asked for a medical timeout. They froze my wrist and taped it up. I picked up my foil again—and dropped it in agony. No way could I continue, unless…

I took advantage of a little-used rule that allows a fencer to change hands if the hand he starts with is disabled. René Roch, the head of the FIE, per-

I took advantage of the little–used rule that lets a fencer switch hands if the hand he starts with is disabled.

sonally gave the referee permission to let me do it.

To my good fortune, Andrey Deev, a Russian fencer, was in the hall, not fencing, but still with his equipment—and it was my size!. I borrowed it all: glove, electric vest, and foil, and went back on the strip.

I lost that bout 13 – 10, but I had fun. I scored four touches in an elite event, fencing right-handed. Looking at it another way, though, it wasn't so good. I couldn't hold a foil in my fencing hand. Still, I and my team had already qualified for the Olympics. Now I had to try to recover.

The following week, something very nice happened to me for a change. I accompanied my student to a Women's World Cup in Tunisia. After the introduction of the final four, the organizers called me onto the strip and presented me with a beautiful silver foil, compliments of the Tunisian Fencing Federation. It was very nice, but strange: the prize was originally to have gone to the winner of the tournament. One of the German trainers asked me whether that would have happened to ValentinaVezzali if she had showed up at a men's World Cup (look her record up and you'll see what he meant). I saw his point, but it still felt great to be honored that way.

The week after that, I went to Turin with my student. There was a women's event, and I didn't fence at all. I couldn't. My wrist still hadn't come around.

I did manage to take a fifth in Seoul, though. My wrist still wasn't' 100%, so I tried to use my legs and my head.

The next week, in China, I took ninth place, losing to Ye Chong 5 – 4 (in a 15-touch bout!) My student was fencing at the exact same time as I was, and during all my breaks, I was watching her instead of trying to stay concentrated.

In the following weeks, my injury and lack of training started to catch up to me in a big way: 33rd in Venice, 17th in Bonn, and again 33rd in Paris.

Thoughts of Retirement

On the bright side, the day before fencing in Paris, I passed the refereeing exam that would allow me to preside at World Championships. I needed a way of staying in the fencing world, which was much too important to me to let go, even though it was increasingly clear that my career was in its final stages.

I had to take care of myself; I had to start thinking about my life after fencing: I had decided to retire after the 2000 Sydney Olympics.

As a young fencer, I had never been able to understand why fencers retired—too early, as I thought, at the age of twenty-seven or thirty. I'm not talking about weak fencers, but the very best: Thorsten Weidner the 1991 World Cup winner, Alex Koch, world champion in 1989 and 1993, Thomas Endres who was second at the 1988 Olympics, Fabio Di Russo, and many others. The reasons had ranged from injuries to loss of confidence. It was sad to see the giants walk away, leaving the fencing world to the merely average. I didn't understand when I was starting out, but now I did.

Even now, in 2004, fencers, coaches, friends, and fans keep asking me when I'll make my comeback. No, I'd made my choice in 2000. I was tired of competing on my own, without my father, without my team, on my own every time, seeing the same cities, the same gyms, the same hotels, the same faces.

Also, none of us gets any younger. My left wrist was no good, my left elbow wasn't that great, and my left knee wasn't much better. And I wasn't training very much anymore. It would add up to more and more frequent defeats.

And I didn't want to lose.

I didn't want the new generation to trample me as I declined.

I wanted to remain a legend in the memory of those who came after me.

*So I had already decided to retire...*when life gave me another jolt: My girlfriend decided to break up with me. Within a few days, she was gone. For the first time in my life, I was alone, a foreigner.

For the next month, wine and cigarettes were my best friends, or so it seemed just then.

My wrist was getting better. I made the final eight in a world cup in Vienna. Before the Olympics, there still remained the world cup in Havana, the European Championships in Madeira, Portugal and the world cup in St. Petersburg for me to tune up. From the end of June to the beginning of August, hope returned. My girlfriend and I were trying to get back together. But just before St. Petersburg, I called her up and heard her final "No."

I got to St. Petersburg the day before the tournament and drank—vodka this time—until two in the morning. I wasn't thinking about the Olympics, about fencing, about the tournament...no, wait.

One lucid thought crept into my mind:

This might be the last World Cup of my career. I was tied with Andrea Borella at seventeen world cup victories. No matter how sorry for myself I was, no matter how badly I hurt, no matter how much I had drunk, if I was going to beat Borella's record, I needed to win in the morning.

Jon Bon Jovi's words from "It's My Life" ran through my head: *Got to make your own breaks*

That was it.

> This might be my last World Cup, my last chance to break Borella's record.
> Bon Jovi's song ran through my mind: *"Got to make your own breaks."*
> It didn't matter how badly I hurt.
> I went to sleep.

I went to bed.

In the morning, I went to the fencing hall. I warmed up, trying to work the alcohol out of my system—trying to make myself feel like an athlete again.

The day of the competition, it was my day. I was winning in good style, fencing easily—no backbreakers, no injuries—despite a tough draw including the best Russian fencers.

The second pitted me against Gerd Salbrechter of Austria, who had beaten me in Venice. The second matched Dmitri Shevchenko against Ilgar Mamedov.

During the few hours' break before the final four, I talked with my old friend and teammate, Ilgar Mamedov. It didn't matter that we might meet in the final. We were old friends together. I told him of my preoccupation: if I won, I would surpass Borella.

On that day, Salbrechter never had a chance against me. It was fast and painless, 15 – 4. In the other semi, Shevchenko beat Mamedov 15 – 13, throwing his foil (as he had tried to do against me) to score the last touch. Ilgar felt the way I did about how friends should fence each other: he was furious with Dmitri.

The final, against Dmitri, was like a one-way street that was running my way, not his. The score was 15 – 6. I had achieved my dream.

This being the year it was, there was a downside to the victory, which I could have foreseen, but didn't. You know how I constantly think about future match-ups. Well, the Olympic table was finally determined by the result at this tournament—and squarely in my path to the Olympic finals, it placed Young-ho Kim, whom I hadn't beaten since Cape Town, and who, to be frank, was very high on my "don't want to fence" list. I could have avoided him by not winning the tournament.

But I wasn't thinking about all that as I entered the finals of that World Cup. And maybe that was a good thing.

In this year of troubles, I also was having problems with my employment in Holland. In the first place, the city of The Hague wanted to build a new building, so it condemned the building where the OKK Club, my employer, had its home. The club got cash compensation, enough to rent new quarters, but not enough to buy a new building. That was the end of morning practice sessions.

In addition, neither of the Dutch fencers I had been training qualified for the Olympics. Indra Angad-Gaur had narrowly failed to qualify, despite achieving four World Cup finals and a world ranking of fifteenth. Paul Sanders hadn't qualified either. That meant that the Netherlands Olympic Committee terminated my contract, effective September.

My coaching income would no longer be enough to support me. My future in Holland was suddenly doubtful.

Help came from my guardian angel Maarten Jansen, the president of my fencing club. OKK established a fund whose interest would supplement my salary.

Also, I'd set up two camps for the Ukrainian team, one in The Hague and the next in Conegliano, Italy, in the Veneto district of Italy northwest of Venice. They were an exciting start for the Golubitsky Fencing Center (about which more later) and promised me an ideal preparation for the Olympics.

Little did I know…

Return to the Twilight Zone

My father, with the Ukrainian team, had boarded a van headed for Rotterdam. Ukraine had no money for hotels, so the team members would be staying with Maarten Jansen, thanks to his generosity. I was sitting in my apartment, waiting for the news that the bus as in. Then I got a sharp reminder that I was still in the Twilight Zone.

The telephone rang, but it wasn't the news of arrival. It

was Alexei Krugliak, one of my father's students.

"Your dad just passed out," he said. "We think it might be a heart attack or a stroke. The ambulance is on its way—"…and then I lost the signal.

I paced frantically back and forth across that little apartment, waiting for more news. It was forty-five minutes before Alexei called again.

"We're in Utrecht," he said, and gave me the address of a hospital. In a minute, I was on the road with my heart pounding, beginning the thirty-mile drive.

It seemed to take forever, but finally I walked into the hospital room. Just at that moment, he regained consciousness. The doctors still had no clue about what had happened to him.

I drove him back to my apartment, where he slept the rest of the day and all that night.

Dad's stroke—for that is what it turned out to be—was triggered by an almost unbelievable incident that seemed to belong in historical fiction. In Poland, the fencers' van had been pursued and overtaken by a gang of modern-day highwaymen, who had tried to cut them off and rob them at gunpoint. Fortunately, Grigori Kriss, Kiev's fencing chief, showed the cool head and fighting spirit that had won him four Olympic medals: he used the van to push the bandits' car aside so that the team could escape down the highway.

> Gangsters had attempted to hijack our fencers' van on a Polish highway. Grigori Kriss had pushed their car aside to let the team escape. My father was badly shaken. Hours later, he had a stroke.

The incident, piled onto weeks of sleepless nights, had badly shaken my father. Hours later, in Holland, he had a stroke (he had another one two years later that forced him to retire from his job as trainer). Before our departure for the second camp, in Conegliano, he confessed to me that he still didn't feel well. The back of his head was numb. He was afraid to go to Italy.

I bought a ticket for him and put him on a plane to Kiev. The camp in Italy was fine, but suddenly my preparation for the Olympics didn't look so ideal anymore.

Ten days or so before the Olympics, I returned to Kiev and received the Order of St. Volodimir from the Ukrainian Orthodox Church for my achievements. My dad was improving and eventually felt well enough to give me a few fencing lessons, which I welcomed for many reasons.

Just before the Olympics, there was a formal sendoff for the Ukrainian athletes at Kiev's biggest concert hall, the beautiful October Palace. All the athletes were onstage. The new Prime Minister was there, as well as numerous politicians, some famous, some not so famous—people who remembered us once every four years and hoped to share our moment of celebrity. Of course the Sports Committee was there too. Their jobs depended on our results, and they'd even been given quotas: three medals for the fencing team, for example. They hadn't asked the athletes or the coaches. Standing on the stage under the gaze of the politicians and officials, I felt like a caged animal in a zoo.

Squirming and trying to hide, I was presented to the Prime Minister as "the best fencer of all time."

"I will personally guard your medals for you," he said.

"I have to win them first," I said drily.

I wasn't happy with the composition of the foil team, either, because politics had stuck its nose in there as well. The three starters—Alexei Bryzgalov, Alexei Krugliak, and I—were all from Dinamo; the alternate, Oleg Matseichuk, was from the Army. It was politically advantageous for Dinamo to dominate the squad. My father was employed by Dinamo and all three Dinamo fencers were his students—a huge feather in his cap. At the same time, it was true that he had been under pressure from above to favor Dinamo fencers in the squad selection. Open competition for the places on the team might have made for a stronger squad, but it was impossible.

We would regret it.

The day of departure for Sydney finally arrived, but there was still no smooth sailing. I was sitting in the departure lounge at Borispol Airport with the other Olympic fencers, waiting to board the airliner for the long flight: Kiev—Frankfurt—Singapore—Sydney—when the Chief of Mission, the team boss, summoned me and two fencers from the women's foil team.

"Your doping tests were positive," he said curtly. "You're staying home. Don't you realize that three positive doping tests from one nation disqualify the entire national team? How could you do this?"

"My testosterone level was high, right?" I asked.

"Right," he said.

"This was all settled back in 1994," I said, almost shouting with frustration. I couldn't believe that our Olympic Committee didn't know about this. "If you don't believe me, I'll take a taxi back to Kiev!"

The Chief of Mission didn't know what to think. He had three athletes with positive doping tests standing in front of him, and all of them came from the same discipline: fencing. That looked bad. On the other hand, I was Ukraine's best fencer, with a long history in international competition. I might be telling the truth...

In the end, he compromised. He let me board the plane, but not the girls, who were now in tears, protesting their innocence.

Later, it turned out that they had been treated by the same doctor, for the same kind of injury, in the same way— some kind of compress whose ingredients had entered their bloodstream. In the midst of their treatment, they'd been asked to take the doping test. They needed a retest badly, but Ukraine lacked the necessary lab. They had to wait for days until their new samples could be flown to

Moscow and the results—all clear!—came back. Only then could they proceed to the Olympics.

The Olympics: Sydney 2000

Once in Sydney, my troubles continued. There was something wrong with my accreditation card, so I couldn't go to the Olympic Village with the rest of the team. I had to wait two hours for a bus, then stand in an endless line waiting for my photo to be taken, then wait for my new card—which in fact was identical to the old one—before finally taking a bus to the Village and wandering around to find the Ukrainian team headquarters.

This Olympic Village seemed smaller and more compact than the one in Atlanta. I was sharing a sort of camper or trailer with my father. The dining hall was a short walk away, as was the recreation center, where I spent a lot of my time meeting other athletes from around the world. I also met one from my past, the rower Anatoli Tishenko from my Dinamo days. We spend some happy time catching up with each other's lives.

I did some sightseeing, but Sydney reminded me too much of my ex-girlfriend.

It was barely beginning to be spring in Sydney, and the nights were freezing, but the temperature warmed up nicely during the day. I did some sightseeing, but Sydney reminded me too much of my ex-girlfriend. Once again, I skipped the opening ceremonies, watching them on TV from the Village. I was thinking about the foil tableau. I already knew that I would meet Young Ho Kim in the quarterfinals—assuming that we both won our first two bouts.

Kim started first. He had a tough bout against Brice Guyart, then a spirited young Frenchman (now the 2004 Olympic champion!) who gave him all he could handle. Despite being behind for most of the bout, Kim pulled it out, 15 – 13.

I wasn't nervous. But that wasn't a good thing.

My first bout was against James Beevers of the UK. I'd never fenced him; I'd just seen him a few times at World Cups As I took my warm-up lesson, I knew that he was watching me. I could see that he was scared.

With that attitude, he didn't have a chance. After a few minutes, I led 14 – 0. I wanted to win 15 – 0, so I made one more attack. Whoops! 14 – 1.

The crowd gave James an ovation. He lifted his arms triumphantly. I took my mask off and gave him an absolutely sincere handshake.

A few second later, it was 15 – 1.

Cliff Bayer was Kim's next opponent. Bayer led 14 – 13, and I was pulling for him hard, not wanting to meet Kim. The score became 14 – 14. Cliff decided to stake everything on his best action. He attacked…Kim ducked and stop thrust…one light…victory for Kim.

I had to fence Matteo Zennaro. I knew that he would never quit, but I was still a little too confident because I had never lost to him. I paid the price when Matteo enjoyed leads of 8 – 2 and 9 – 3.

At that point, I started to fight. No more elegance: it was much more like a street brawl. I cut into his lead, one touch at a time, and finally won 15 – 12.

Now it was time to meet Kim. I'd known his great potential for years and had been surprised that he hadn't started to achieve top results until 1996 – 1997, when I barely beat him in the World Championships in Cape Town. In 1999, he'd won the bronze in the World Championships. One newspaper was to write of him, "He combines a Latin temperament with European toughness and Asian concentration." We had met three times in 1997, and he had the advantage over me, two bouts to one.

I didn't want to fence him (not that I had a choice), but I

wasn't' scared of him. I had a great plan for the bout.

I started off well, following my plan, fencing on the tactical defensive. Soon enough, I led 4 – 1.

"Why not attack?" I said to myself. Point against, 4 – 2.

"Let's get it back," I said to myself, making another attack. 4 – 3.

I threw my great plan out the window, making one senseless attack after another. My strongest weapon, my analytical ability, deserted me completely. By the time I realized what was happening, I was so far behind that I would have to attack if I wanted to catch up.

> My analytical ability deserted me. I made one senseless attack after another. I couldn't hear. I couldn't listen. I couldn't do anything.

Off-target. Off-target. Flat. Off-target. Flat.

My dad was screaming something at me, but I couldn't hear him. I couldn't listen. I couldn't do anything anymore until the bout was over: 15 – 5.

It was Kim's easiest bout of the Olympics. He had a much tougher time later on, beating Shevchenko and Bissdorf by identical scores of 15 – 14 to achieve Olympic gold.

I slunk back to our camper in the Village. My father was there before me. Carefully, he poured to plastic glasses of cognac and handed one to me.

"We still love you, son," he said. We drank.

It was the sweetest thing I had ever heard from him.

Two days after my debacle in the individuals came the team event. I was totally depressed, but strangely, my negative thoughts vanished as soon as I put my mask on and gripped my weapon. The team event was now my only thought, the last big goal in my fencing career.

There were only eight teams in the event, and the first

match would separate the top four from the rest. We fenced Italy and trailed from the outset. I didn't start so well, losing my first bout 5 – 3 and drawing the next, 5 – 5. When I faced Toti Sanzo in the last bout, we were behind 40 – 29, and he hit me twice at the outset, making it 42 – 29. I had to score sixteen points before he could score three, and all in less than three minutes.

And I almost did it. I found my rhythm and turned on the afterburners. The score reached 44 – 40 with plenty of time left. My teammates started to believe in miracles.

But Toti found time for a counterattack. Italy won, 45 – 40, and went on to take the bronze medal. Ukraine was relegated to the bottom half of the draw.

Our next opponent was Russia, which had lost to China for the top four. They were demoralized and we were still hungry, winning big, 45 – 37.

Our final match was against Germany. Beforehand, both teams waited in a little room. I told them that this was the last team match of my career.

Germany was leading 40 – 34 when I faced Sydney's silver medalist, Ralf Bissdorf, in the final bout. I beat him 11 – 3, bringing victory to our team, 45 – 43. We placed fifth, which I think was an extraordinary result for our team and one that will not soon be equaled.

I was changing after the match when Ralf Bissdorf came up to me, camera in hand, asking for a picture. He had tears in his eyes.

"Cheer up," I said. "You Germans have a lot of medals left in you."

> "I'm crying because you're retiring, and because I'm proud to have been your opponent."

"That's not it," he said. "I'm crying because you're retiring from fencing, and because I'm proud to have been your last opponent."

"Stop it," I told him, "or I'll be crying too!"

That evening, I went to Austrian House for "a beer" with my friend Benny Wendt. Despite the free flow of spirits and the funny stories that we shared, there was an undertone of sorrow. I got sadder and sadder. A few days later, Ilgar Mamedov tried to cheer me up about my loss.

"It's not the loss," I told him. "It's our last time."

It was true. Ilgar and Dmitri Shevchenko were going to retire also. It was the last time for all of us. We had given twenty years of our lives, and more, to competitive fencing; we had beaten and lost to each other and shared each other's victories and defeats. Now we had all reached the end of the road.

The next moment, I was trying to cheer up Ilgar.

Back in Ukraine, the Olympic Committee would decide that the foil team had achieved unsatisfactory results. They fired my father.

> I had to figure out how to start a new life. Without competitive fencing.

That was how they rewarded his years of dedicated work and his many successes.

As for me, I had to go back to Holland and think how to start a new life.

Without competitive fencing.

I would be starting over.

Again…

Life After Life

As it happened, I didn't quit right away. I tried, but the pull of fencing was too strong.

During the Olympics, I received an e-mail from a Dutch friend, Paula Papilaja, telling me of a vacancy for a gym teacher in her home town, Breda. It wasn't something I looked forward to, but I didn't have much of a choice. My failure at the Sydney Olympics had led to a halving of my monthly salary from Ukraine: I would be making about US $100.00 a month, hardly enough for me to live on, not to mention my obligation to pay child support for my daughter and help my parents out. The combined salaries from the OKK Club and the teaching job in Breda offered me some hope.

Going into the interview, I had some serious liabilities. I had absolutely no experience as a schoolteacher, and my Dutch was far from perfect. I got the job, but it was a disaster from Day One. The conditions weren't bad and the salary was good, but I couldn't control the kids. (I was used to the discipline of the fencing hall.) I lasted six months, then spoke with the principal and quit with a deep sense of relief.

Life without fencing was colorless and boring. Despite my decision to quit, I started coming to the OKK gym an hour early, just to train again. The harder I trained, the more I punished my body, the better I felt.

But I *was* punishing my body. Even before the

Olympics, I had become conscious of a pain in my right heel, but I ignored it. Now it forced itself on my attention: my first few steps each morning were agonizing. No big deal, I told myself. I was training for Paris, for my favorite competition. I was setting out once again on the road to the Olympics. I knew that the decision would please my father. I was happy.

While training for Paris, I received a letter. It said something about a jury, a sports jury. I didn't understand. Then I remembered.

It was at that last, sad party at Austria House, near the end of the Olympics. The journalist Wolfgang Eichler had been excited about some project that he said he had in mind for me. I hadn't paid attention to "Wolfy" at the time; I was too busy saying goodbye to fencing. Now it was clear.

Wolfy had managed to get me onto the World Jury for the World Sports Awards of the Twentieth Century. There were one hundred and fifty of us, and we each got the names of seventy-five nominees. The chairman of the jury was Juan Antonio Samaranch, the head of the International Olympic Committee.

And on the jury—

Forgive me if I drop some names here. I was stunned, and remain stunned, dizzy, dazzled, and amazed to think of myself in the company of so many people I had admired all my life....

...people like boxing great Muhammad Ali, long jumper Bob Beamon, soccer immortal Sir Bobby Charlton, gymnast Nadia Comaneci, motorcycle racer Michael Doohan, tennis players Steffi Graf and Pat Cash, the Norwegian speed skater Johann Olav Koss, Austrian Formula One race car driver Niki Lauda, sailor HRH Prince Albert de Monaco, and so many more.

The first night of the event was a celebration of Muhammad Ali's fifty-ninth birthday. The second night was held at the Royal Albert Hall in London and hosted

Life After Life

by Roger Moore of James Bond fame. I met some people I already knew: Russian gymnast Alexei Nemov, Ukrainian swimmer Jana Klochkova, Dutch cyclist Leontien Zijlaard-van Moorsel, Italian fencer Valentina Vezzali and, of course, Wolfgang "Wolfy" Eichler, to whom I owed a debt of gratitude for getting me here.

Let me mention even more of the world's greatest athletes whom I met on this occasion: US sprinter Michael Johnson, Dutch swimmers Inge De Bruijn and Pieter van den Hoogenband and Dutch footballer Ruud Gullit, Czech javelin thrower Jan Zelezny, world heavyweight champion Lennox Lewis, and Austrian skier Herman Maier. Afterwards, there was a charity auction at which, I remember, a 1969 photo of Muhammad Ali sold for US $15,000.

The actual awards were presented the next evening, Oscar-style. I sat next to Sir Bobby Charlton, at the same table as Pál Schmitt, the former Olympic epee gold medalist who was now Hungarian Ambassador to Switzerland.

At the end of the evening, the "All-Star Band," consisting of John McEnroe, Bryan Adams, Daemon Hill, and Eddie Jordan, sang "We Gonna Win."

It was an unforgettable evening that inspired me for Paris. Getting there was a thrill. People crowded around me, thanking me...for coming back to fence.

No, thank *you*, all of you!

Philippe Omnès even asked me whether I was going to fence right-handed again!

I took fifth and had a blast.

But the pain in my heel was getting worse. I tried to bull my way through it, but it wouldn't let up. It got so that if I went out running, I had to limp back after fifty meters. The doctors advised me to get a special orthotic insole, but I ignored them. At the same time, I had to quit training.

Nevertheless, I was getting discouraged. The Olympics were almost four years away—could I go on that long? My father was no longer the Ukraine's foil coach; that was discouraging, too. I started to weigh my life on a pair of

245

Among the Immortals ...

With Norwegian Speed Skater Johann Olav Koss (L.)

With Czech Javelin Thrower Jan Zelezny (R.)

With English Soccer Immortal Sir Bobby Charlton (L.)

With Dutch Soccer Great Ruud Gullit (L.)

imaginary scales. On one side was my Olympic dream, my twenty years of competitive fencing, my whole life up till now; on the other side was my real life right now, with all its worries and problems. And that side seemed to become heavier day by day.

The Golubitsky Fencing Center is Born

In the year 2000, a bright idea for my future life came from my American student, Daniel Boles: start my own training center. That was how GFC—the Golubitsky Fencing Center—was born.

Daniel had an interesting story of his own. Born in Palo Alto, California, in the heart of Silicon Valley, he followed his father into computer programming. He was financially successful, but his heart yearned for excitement. He took up the daredevil sport of motocross and became good at it—as good as you can be while holding down a full-time job. He had a high regional ranking, but the top pros were a half-step ahead of him. Again and again, he felt that he was about to take that extra half-step, and maybe more, but luck, like a desert mirage, kept eluding him.

It was Daniel's career that sent him to Singapore to work for Hewlett-Packard; but it must have been fate that made him cross the threshold of Singapore's "Z" Fencing Club and almost instantaneously get hooked on our sport. While in Singapore, he watched the video of my final against Young Ho Kim in Cape Town. That was his first acquaintance.

A manager from HP's Netherlands office happened to be in Singapore. As fate would have it, he recruited Daniel to come join his team in Europe. A few weeks later, my phone rang while I was in the middle of giving a lesson. A guy with an American accent was asking whether he could train with me. That's the short story of how we met.

Daniel is four years older than I am. It was too late for him to think about a world-class career in fencing. But for

the next two years, "D," as I call him, led the life of a professional fencer. I called him the most professional amateur in
the world.

In the summer of 2000, I gave my first international
camp. It was for the Singapore fencers, Daniel's clubmates.
Right afterwards, D came up with the idea of GFC, and
without informing me, he started to build the website.
Chris Geurts, a designer, created a beautiful logo. Chris
was the father of my student Djinn, then a girl of twelve,
but today, in 2004, the senior Dutch champion while still a
cadet! The concept, the website, and the logo were all wonderful gifts.

I warmed to the idea rapidly. The concept was to or-
ganize training camps for fencers. This way I could help
people who shared my passion.

I mentioned already that just before the Olympics, I'd
organized two camps for the Ukrainian foil team. (That
was before my father and the Ukrainian team were nearly
hijacked on the way to Holland.)

After the turmoil was over, these camps provided
the impetus and inspiration for the Golubitsky Fencing
Center.

The GFC Idea

I'd coached in quite a variety of fencing situations:
Austria, Holland, Italy.

Austria offered great working conditions, but too many
of the fencers I worked with had the wrong mentality.
Austria has a superb competitive mentality—for skiing.
Turn on a TV in Austria and you will see an Austrian kick-
ing butt on the slopes. Go to a fencing club and you will
see…an Austrian thinking about his skiing. At least, that's
how I felt. At that club, at that time, the students I worked
with weren't prepared to be serious about fencing.

In Holland, on the other hand, I had some students with
a perfect mentality for fencing. The problem was that start-

ing in 2000, when the city dispossessed our fencing club, it was only possible to give four training sessions a week.

In Conegliano, Italy, I live and work in a lovely location near the mountains and not, I thought, too far from Venice. Besides that, Italy is one of the world's perennial fencing giants. But here I have found it difficult to convince my students that they could really win. They were afraid to pit themselves against the fencers from the powerhouse clubs. I need to make them believe, go for it all out—and maybe win.

That's why my friend Daniel and I came up with the idea of the Golubitsky Fencing Center.

Suppose you are a really passionate fencer. You want to learn more. You believe that one person—you—could make a difference.

But your country doesn't have a strong fencing program. Or it does, but you are too far from the powerhouses.

The GFC concept is to run camps that will give you the *insight and consciousness* that come from a top program: sharp sparring, top coaching, devoted practice…

So GFC brings that powerhouse fencing program to you. For the period of the camp, you are trained as an elite fencer in a world-class program.

… and the *special ways of seeing*, of reading the opponent and the situation that seem to be inborn in elite fencers but are really the result of training.

At GFC, I stress the mentality of a top fencer. For a few examples, see the box on the next page:

The GFC Mentality:

- You will make mistakes, but you must not allow yourself to make the same mistake twice.
- Between the referee's halt and the command to fencer, you have between five and ten seconds to analyze the situation, recognize your mistakes, and prepare the solution for the next touch.
- Finish your action faster than you started it. The lunge must be faster than the advance, the riposte must be faster than the parry.
- You will learn a wide spectrum of actions and how to apply them at the right distance. Then you will learn how to read the opponent in order to select the right action to perform.

After a week or ten days of GFC, you won't be a world champion (unless you were already close when you came!) But GFC will give you the *foundation* for better fencing and the *road map* for getting there.

You can find out more, including how to arrange for a clinic, at the GFC website: www.gfc-world.com

Thoughts on Coaching

Ihad started my coaching career late in 1996, after the Atlanta Olympics. I had the good fortune to work with many different ages and levels of fencers, young beginners to elite professionals, middle-aged amateurs. I've worked with fencers from many different countries and cultures: Singapore, the United States, Great Britain, Mexico, Finland, Ukraine, Holland, France, Italy, Switzerland, New Zealand, Indonesia, and Spain. I've made my mistakes, learned from them, and evolved my own way of teaching based on the classic schools I've learned from, the many fine coaches I've worked with, and my still-evolving experience.

The mark of a good trainer, a good head coach, is the ability to fencers at a sufficiently high level over a period of time. To do this, a trainer has to be in constant search mode, looking for new techniques, new tactical solutions, new training methods.

We live in a world of change and sport is changing with it. Fencing today is different from what it was fifty years ago, which was different from what it was a hundred years ago: there are new rules, new materials, new training methods, and a lot more. A trainer has to change simply to keep up.

At the same time, it is essential for the trainer to be faithful to his own style and vision. If you teach one way today, a different way next Monday and still a third way the following month, if you don't have understanding and confidence in the way you do things, you'll fail—as measured by your athletes and their results. If your students leave you for another coach, you have to ask yourself why. Was it force of circumstances (change of address, injury), was it external pressure—or was it something you did? If it was the latter, have the guts to admit it, and then find new ways to improve.

But don't stop your students from working with other trainers, especially if you have to admit to yourself that you can't bring the fencer to the next level by yourself. It's not fair to hold your fencer back, and you may learn something from the experience.

As a trainer, you have to understand the mentality, the psychology, the spirit of your fencer. Fencing is a mental game.

Look at the top, let's say sixty-four fencers in the world. They have more or less the same physical, technical, and tactical abilities. But only a few will ever be champions; the rest will remain in the "he was a pretty strong fencer" category. Some fencers are invincible in practice, but only a few are invincible, even for a while, at the tournament.

And what's the difference? Mentality.

Your job as trainer, then, is slowly and carefully to *mold the mentality* of your fencer. If you can do this, you can proudly claim to take part in an act of magic. You can share in your student's victory.

And this is what I try to get across in every session of GFC.

One student's picture of how I coach follow is in the box on the following page:

Fencing at a GFC Center

You are standing on a line next to 20 other fencers in descending order from tallest to shortest (it seems that with Golubitsky even something as common as a lineup presents the need to quickly analyze something - in this case who is taller and shorter than you).

"Who wants a lesson?" he asks. Nervously, you raise your hand, as do many others, half-hoping you get picked, and half-hoping you don't. It is a chance to make serious progress, yet it is also a gut wrenching session requiring absolute focus combined with the ability to flow and relax—while being subjected to a constant stream of corrections on seemingly minute details.

As Golubitsky's student, you must be ready to do precisely and immediately what you are told to do, and yet be sufficiently observant, flexible, and balanced to improvise or fall back on an earlier learned routine if Sergei gives an unexpected trigger with blade or movement.

On the worst of days, the barrage of corrections can render you catatonic. In the best of lessons, everything seems to come together with clarity and feeling, and you may even get an occasional "yes, yes, good"...at which time you know you've made a serious step forward as a fencer. It can be bitterly difficult at times; it is to the same extent inspiring and motivating. And even on the bad days, when everything seems to be going wrong, you know that what you are being shown is relevant and that eventually it will work its way into your fencing and provide you with one more way to land touches.

What's special about Golubitsky's lessons is not just that you are working with a great champion and talented coach, but that you wind up doing a large number of techniques with full understanding of the subtle details that make them work. The attention to detail can seem extreme, but when you see a top fencer doing a lesson with him, or see him taking a lesson from his father Vitali, it all makes sense.

I asked him once, "What is the most important thing that a developing fencer should do?" He replied, "It isn't always about what the fencer should do. Coaches need to make sure they don't skip steps in developing their fencers. And the fencers, they need to always be doing their homework and analyzing their own fencing, strengths and weaknesses and why." Through my time training with Golubitsky, I can certainly confirm his words match with his day in, day out training.

—Daniel Boles

Last World Cup in Venice

But first, there was Venice, and another World Cup. Daniel had never been there, and I told myself I wanted to show him the glories of the city.

I almost couldn't fence. The Ukrainian Federation had paid for my international license, but somehow I hadn't received it; and similarly, Ukraine hadn't sent in my registration form. The FIE was getting strict about these things.

Fine, I said. I'll spend my time in Venice as a tourist. (I was serious.)

The organizers wouldn't allow it. They waived the rules to let me fence. I am grateful to them, and to Jean-Claude Blondeau of France, the FIE official who gave the final OK.

I was exhausted after the first bout, thanks to a month without training. After the second, I was in agony. Fencing almost on one leg, I made the final four. There was a break.

I made my decision.

During the break, I went to the organizers and asked them to announce publicly that that this World Cup would be the last in my career. The crowd cheered me, and I took them to my heart. From that moment on, we were as one. This one was for them.

Before my semifinal bout against Slawomir Mocek of Poland, I sat alone and prayed to God. I offered Him my fencing career—I'd end it on the spot—if He would grant me victory in this one last tournament.

The bout started badly. I was down 6 – 1 and 8 – 3. The pain wasn't unbearable as long as I was fencing, but it came back in waves every time the referee called a halt.

Just before time ran out, I tied the score at thirteen. Mocek won the coin toss and priority, which meant that I had to find a way to attack. I won on a double-beat attack, 14 – 13.

And now came the final—the real final: the finale of my fencing career, against Christian Schlechtweg of Germany.

I felt relaxed and at peace, fencing to create beauty, making difficult actions look simple. Victory was mine, 15 – 9, and I shared it to the full with the spectators.

I stood on the podium, holding the beautiful Murano glass vase, the prize for victory. It was my third triumph in Venice. I had ended my career with my nineteenth World Cup win—breaking my own record. I could not have asked for a finer ending.

Daniel and I stirred up the funk that night in celebration, in Venice, that amazing city.

Finally, I was happy that it was over.

> I was happy that it was over. Now I could dedicate myself to my students instead of stealing time from them.

I was happy that I didn't *have* to fence any more; I didn't have to run, to train, to strive for the next height. I looked forward to enjoying the role of spectator, of coach… Yes, there was a lot I was looking forward to as a coach. Now I could dedicate myself fully to my students instead of stealing time from them.

What had really tipped the balance for me, though, was this: more and more often, I caught myself thinking *how not to lose*, instead of *how to win*. For me, that was a sure sign that it was time to go.

Suddenly, I felt sorry for my dad. Now that I saw myself as a coach, I could understand the sorrow of his position: year after year, for one reason and another, all his students sooner or later leave the sport, while he goes on. It's a little death for a coach or trainer to see a student walk away after he gave that student his heart and soul. I knew that my decision to quit had stolen a piece of my father's dream.

I didn't know for sure where my life would take me. The only thing I was sure of was that I would never leave fencing, my sport, which had brought me so much joy as well as pain. It made no sense to ask whether I still loved it or not. It was like the air around me—imperceptible when it was there, excruciating whenever it was absent.

Yes, part of me hated fencing: the injuries, the embarrassments over doping, the defeats (every one of them), the demands of training and tournaments, which deprived me of a normal life.

But still I loved it: there were the intense, joyous moments of victory, the world travel, the deep friendships, the satisfaction of bringing honor to my country, Ukraine, an independent country for the first time in its history, the satisfaction of being a role model for young fencers the way Smirnov was a role model for me...

There was an omen awaiting me when I got back to Rotterdam: a letter inviting me to referee at the Cadet and Junior World Championships in Gdansk, Poland. It was a great honor—and a perfect transition.

And the best part of it was that one of my Dutch students, Sebastiaan Borst, would be fencing there! Referees get only their expenses paid, but it would be worth it for a chance to watch my student.

Now that I was retired, I finally got around to seeing a doctor for my injury. I chose the sports doctor for the Dutch Olympic Team, Dr. Peter Vergouwen, whom I had first met at the World University Games when I was coaching for the Netherlands. I thought of him as plain "Doc," like the character in "Back to the Future." His explanations were so clear and simple that he made you feel that you understood your own case as well as any professor of medicine. We did X-rays, but they were inconclusive. Dr. Vergouwen ordered me an MRI and managed to get one for me within two weeks, cutting through the usual endless waiting.

Early in April 2001, the day before I was set to go to Gdansk for the World Juniors, I had an appointment with him. He showed me the pictures from the MRI.

"It's a stress fracture," he said. "You have two choices: go for surgery, or take a long rest."

"How long does it take to recover from surgery?"

"Two to three months."

"What is the recovery like?"

"Restricted walking—no driving."

It was the middle of the fencing season for my students as fencers and for me as a referee. I could wait until the summer, but I'd be giving four training camps: one in Holland, two in the US, and one in Britain. I'd have to give those up and spend the summer recovering in my apartment.

No good.

"I'll rest," I told him.

Refereeing

It was time to start my career as a referee. I arrived in Gdansk to general amazement, having exchanged my fencing whites for the referee's dark suit and tie.

I could hardly believe the transformation myself. As a fencer, I had accepted the referee as a necessary evil. If he made the right call, that was normal. I gave myself credit for making the action clear. If he made a mistake, I would lean on him, play games with his head: I'd be a little rude, or I'd by chatty and friendly. In short, I'd try to influence the referee to give the calls in my favor.

This is part of fencing. If the fencer doesn't do it, the team captain or the coach does it for him. It's a kind of art form: lean on the judge just enough so that he doesn't get mad at you and start to rob you.

Now I was the referee, the one whose mistake could destroy a fencer's hopes and his coach's labor. The shoe was on the other foot. I'm pretty confident about anything concerning fencing, so I was surprised to feel butterflies in my stomach on the first day of women's foil. I could hardly watch the action on the strip! My fellow referees had to do a lot to support me and cheer me up.

Refereeing: "Don't Mess with Me"
(Photo by G. Minozzi)

Giving a Lesson

In Venice with Daniel Boles
after My Last World Cup Victory (Venice, 2000)

My Student, Sebastiaan Borst, with His Medal
Cadet World Championships, Gdansk 2001

I grew more secure from bout to bout, but still it was a surprise when I was called to judge the final four. I didn't know whether to dance for joy or look for the nearest exit.

At the strip, I felt myself strangling inside my referee's tie. The FIE officials and many of the trainers were waiting, watching me, looking for demeanor, ability to read and understand fencing actions, resistance to pressure, control of the bout and, of course, accuracy and honesty.

Meanwhile, the day approached when my student would fence in the Cadet Men's Foil. I hardly had time to watch him because I was refereeing.

Sebastiaan made it through to the final four, assuring himself of a bronze medal. I was delighted. I was sure, too, that I'd get to watch him: surely I wouldn't be asked to referee my own student. But the Directoire Technique named me and two other judges.

I was hand judge in Sebastiaan's semifinal bout against a Polish boy. The Polish boy was constantly on the edge of using his unarmed hand. I knew that if I called him on it, the Polish crowd would show its strong disapproval.

The Polish boy covered. I raised my hand. Yellow card against the Polish boy.

"Sergei, what are you doing?" shouted the Polish coach.

The action resumed. The Polish boy covered. I raised my hand again. Red card.

It had been harder to make the correct call in favor of my fencer than it would have been to make a correct call against him.

Sebastiaan lost by a few touches, winning the bronze medal. I was proud of him and of his achievement.

I was proud, too—as a former fencer who had scored as a trainer.

As a referee, I set a goal for myself: not just to change the way foil was refereed, but to change the way that fencers understood the foil discipline.

In my view, as well as that of other elite fencers, foil was losing its distinctive character and becoming too close to sabre. Specifically, the right of way, or priority of the attack, was being corrupted. It

> My goal in becoming a referee was to change the way in which fencers understood the essence of foil.

was increasingly possible for a fencer merely to walk forward, without threatening his opponent, and still be awarded the right of way against a timely counterattack. The Referees' Commission of the FIE had been trying to clean up foil since 1996, and I thought that I could help.

A few years later, people were telling me that I had made a difference. When I started refereeing even a correctly executed attack on preparation would never get a call—if you pardon my exaggeration. When I finally took a break from refereeing, a few years later, even an incorrectly executed attack on preparation had a chance! Maybe I had made my point too well.

After Gdansk, I continued to expand my work as a trainer. I took on the job of coaching a group of Finnish fencers, mostly in their thirties and forties. Twice a month, I'd fly to Helsinki to coach them. They weren't elite athletes, but the hunger in their eyes inspired me. In the summer, my student Joren van der Voort won bronze in the Dutch Championships, and my students won the team event as well.

The rest of the summer of 2001, I was giving training camps. Most of the fencers weren't elite, but we all had a lot of fun. My purpose was to show them technique and tactics, and most of all to make them understand that fencing isn't a matter of luck and strength, but a duel of fencing intentions that relies on analysis and brainwork. Sometimes, despite my injury, I'd fence my students, whipping my mask off after a touch to explain that the point that I'd just scored had been prepared much earlier.

The Torch is Passed

In late October 2001, in Nîmes, France, the World Championship in Men's Foil finally passed out of my hands. I had held it longer than anyone else on record, for just over four years. I wasn't fencing, that day, of course; I was refereeing. In fact, I was refereeing the bout in which I "lost" the title, when Toti Sanzo dramatically defeated Loic Attely!

I hugged Toti and congratulated him; he told me that he was honored to be my successor. A few days later, Loic (a future team World Champion) told me that I had been his fencing hero.

It's inevitable—the torch has to be passed. I was proud and satisfied to pass it on under those circumstances.

I did compete one more time, though—in 2002, at the Dutch Team Championship, helping my students take the title. A week before, my student Boaz Aronson had won his first ever bronze in the individuals.

Right after that, I made a very hard decision—after living and working in Holland for five years, I would be moving to Conegliano, Italy, where I had held my camp a few years before.

Some of my students had quit fencing, putting my coaching career in Holland in jeopardy through no fault of their own. Others would be coming with me to Conegliano to continue training with me.

I'd be starting all over once again. Jon Bon Jovi's words echoed in my head again: *It's my life—It's now or never...I just want to live while I'm alive!*

Reflections: Fencing and the Athlete

What is Fencing?

Fencing is the art of
1) *Analyzing* the situation.
2) *Deciding* what action is necessary to score.
3) *Executing* the needed action
    (technique, conditioning, etc.).

Yes, it's that simple, *but...*

Analysis requires careful study of your opponent, sometimes with only a very short time available. This gives you the ability to read his intentions and anticipate his actions. Then you can start to set traps.

Of course, two can play that game. One of my opponents once said, about fencing me:

"Sometime I think I've set him up perfectly. Then, at the last moment, when it's already too late, I realize that *he* was setting *me* up, and I'm already in the trap!"

The next step is *decision-making*—or rather, making the *right* decision. In the long-ago age of dueling, you couldn't afford a mistake because your life depended on your judgment. The art of making the right decision today depends on mental conditioning and feedback—your coach drilling you over and over again in how to respond in a variety of situations, as well as the way you use your own experience on the fencing strip.

Last, and most difficult, comes *execution.* You can have the analytical genius of a chess master; you can be as decisive as any CEO, but you still have to *execute the action at the right time and distance, using the chosen technique.* That is what people call the "feeling" or the "gift" for the sport, but it is the result of dedicated training and commitment. Just as drops of water can wear down stone, thousands of repetitions can form a winning mentality and lead to perfect execution.

After all that, I have to add that you need to be lucky, too. But "luck is the residue of design:" the better your planning and preparation, the more likely you are to be lucky.

Preparation is the main thing. I used to tell my students, "In fencing, the first fifteen years are the hardest!" They'd look at me, startled—then realize that I was joking.

But there's a truth in the joke.

It doesn't matter that you are making the same stupid mistake again and again—if you are prepared to learn. I walked down that same road. Keep going and you'll get there. It took me fifteen years to reach my highest level.

Why Fencing is Great

Finally, let me say a few words about the *essence* of fencing. What is its special quality; what gives it its beauty and uniqueness? What are its differences, its advantages, over other sports?

To put it another way, what aspects of fencing can we use to reach out and bring people into our wonderful sport?

Let's leave team sports out of it. Team sports depend on the interaction of the players, and even among top professionals, only a very small percentage—a Michael Jordan, a Pélé, a Maradona—have the transcendent ability to change a match's outcome on their own. They are the exceptions to the rule, the individuals who transcend the game by their ability. For everyone else, team sports are not the place for individual self-expression.

Sports like gymnastics and figure skating look more like individual contests. But the athletes don't compete against the clock or an opponent; they simply repeat routines that they have learned in advance and rehearsed countless times down to the smallest detail. These sports are about performance, not competition.

In motor sports, the driver is dependent on the quality of his car, his engineers, and his pit crew, not only on his own level of skill.

Swimming, skiing, weightlifting, track and field—these are truly competitions and tests of skill, but not *against* the opponent. Instead, the barrier is the clock, the weight, or the height of the bar.

In tennis and similar sports, you are directly facing an opponent, but across a net.

When we get to wrestling, boxing, judo, tae kwan do, we are getting closer to the mark. But the results often depend on innate qualities of strength and power, although weight classes even things out somewhat.

You see where I'm going: fencing is the perfect sport, the best sport on earth, *because it's a direct physical confrontation with your opponent, but the result is not achieved by mere force, brute strength, or superior equipment.* Fencers must have the qualities that athletes in other

> Fencing is a direct physical confrontation, but brute strength, raw speed, or superior equipment don't decide the outcome.

sports possess: speed and endurance (track and field), power (Olympic weightlifting), coordination and flexibility (gymnastics), quick reactions (boxing, table tennis), special footwork (tennis), and many others

And on top of all these physical gifts, the fencer has to have a mind that can analyze the problem and deliver the solution in split seconds. A trained fencer can *choose* a parry—and a riposte—for the opponent's attack *before someone without training can realize that the attack is on its way!*

But no *one or two* of these qualities is enough to dominate a fencing bout. Why? Because even though we're in combat, we're not in direct body contact with our opponent. We apply all our qualities—we apply ourselves—*through the weapon.* The weapon is the equalizer—that and the will of the fencer. You can lack one, or two, or even more of these qualities—and still use your willpower, your inner strength, to combine the qualities you have and defeat your opponent.

Finally, fencing is based on the principle of defending our own lives—but even more importantly, of defending honor. Fencing remembers that we defend our own honor, the honor of the lady of our heart, the honor of our country.

Hey, I know that a lot of people will think this is all nonsense!

It's my opinion about the beauty of my sport.

Pick up a foil and let's discuss it!

The Athlete

The role of the athlete in modern society is very special. He doesn't primarily produce material value (even if he's paid millions and keeps dozens of people employed). Instead, he produces *morale* for his society—the pride of the people on whose behalf he competes.

There is nothing like the pride of achieving victory for your club, your city, your country, your people. Even in the great athletic nations like the United States or Russia: there is nothing like the shared thrill of seeing your country's flag rise in victory; and there is nothing like the pride that your people have in the victory of one of their own.

This is especially true for small countries, poor countries, or new countries like my Ukraine. When the USSR ceased to exist, fifteen "new" nations appeared on the map, many of them previously unknown to most of the world (despite rich histories, in many cases).

Look at Ukraine. It's a thousand years old, but what do most people around the world know about it besides the Chernobyl disaster and Chicken Kiev? So it's a great thing for all Ukrainians when a Ukrainian athlete becomes world-famous, an example for children, and a standard-bearer for his country, an Ambassador of Sport?

Even the citizens of mega-countries—Americans, Russians, Chinese—feel a surge of pride when their athletes top the world.

Ultimately, what is the reward for the individual—medals, prizes, money, glory?

Sure. But these are external motivations. I think, though, that the ultimate motivator is the *respect* and *recognition* that you can get from your fellow athletes and from other people.

I've had that recognition—as a person, a fencer, a trainer, and a referee. I wish the same success to you, my reader.

Epilogue

The Greek philosopher Pythagoras said that a man should do four things in his lifetime: build a house, plant a tree, father a child, and write a book.

My competitive fencing career was the house I built.

My Fencing Center and my coaching career are the tree that I planted, which will bear fruit for years to come.

My beloved daughter is the child I fathered.

And this is my book.

I never won Olympic gold. But let me tell you about my golden moment.

It was after one of my favorite tournaments, the CIP World Cup in Paris. A Frenchman, a man I didn't know, had been watching my fencing. He came up to me and said these words:

"Sergei, if ever you have no place to live, no roof above your head, no job, just find me and I will help you"

His name: Xavier Boissoye.

Thank you, Xavier. These words are my gold medal.

My Favorite Event—the CIP Tournament in Paris,
before an Expert Crowd of 5,000